MW01201180

TEXAS TEST PREP

8th GRADE STAAR MATH WORKBOOK

SAVITA MAHESHWARI

Revised Edition 2021: 2020 was been an unprecedented year for all of us. The world as we knew it, got disrupted, uprooted and handed back upside down. Yet, all of us have marched on bravely in face of this adversity and created our own measures to deal with the aftermath of the pandemic.

Education has probably been impacted the most - with parents, students and teachers all trying to grapple with the best way to maintain continuity in our learning process. Keeping this in mind, the 2021 edition of this book has been reviewed and analyzed to ensure that it meets the needs of any changes that might have come into the learning process. We've ensured the relevance, timeliness and quality of all the contents so that you may find that at least one thing has remain unchanged - the quality that our students expect from us.

Copyright by Smart Math Tutoring.

All rights reserved. This book or any portion thereof may not be reproduced or used in any manner whatsoever without the express written permission of the Smart Math Tutoring

Preface

This practice workbook contains a comprehensive review of STAAR Exam. The questions in this book are styled for the standardized STAAR exam. With regular practice in solving these questions, the student will feel more confident and better equipped to tackle challenging problems.

About the Author

Savita Maheshwari

Founder of Smart Math Tutoring in Plano, Texas, Savita Maheshwari, is an educator with 12+ years of experience. She has also held the position of an Associate College Professor in a reputed engineering college in India. An Electronics & Communications Engineer turned math teacher, she has a proven record of instilling in her students' a deep love for the subject along with improving their performance on the grade sheet. Her passion and rich experience in teaching are reflected in her classroom and course material. She believes in developing a valuable mental ability, making Math more interesting for students and improving their conceptual and thinking skills. Because of her talent and commitment, she has received love and respect from a large community of students and their parents. Now, she has distilled her years of experience into a series of publications making sure it holds the best content a student can find to improve their math skills.

STAAR GRADE 8 MATHEMATICS REFERENCE MATERIALS

LINEAR EQUATIONS

Slope-intercept form	$y = mx + b$
Direct variation	$y = kx$
Slope of a line	$m = \dfrac{y_2 - y_1}{x_2 - x_1}$

CIRCUMFERENCE

Circle	$C = 2\pi r$	or	$C = \pi d$

AREA

Triangle	$A = \dfrac{1}{2}bh$
Rectangle or parallelogram	$A = bh$
Trapezoid	$A = \dfrac{1}{2}(b_1 + b_2)h$
Circle	$A = \pi r^2$

SURFACE AREA

	Lateral	Total
Prism	$S = Ph$	$S = Ph + 2B$
Cylinder	$S = 2\pi rh$	$S = 2\pi rh + 2\pi r^2$

VOLUME

Prism or cylinder	$V = Bh$
Pyramid or cone	$V = \dfrac{1}{3}Bh$
Sphere	$V = \dfrac{4}{3}\pi r^3$

ADDITIONAL INFORMATION

Pythagorean theorem	$a^2 + b^2 = c^2$
Simple interest	$I = Prt$
Compound interest	$A = P(1 + r)^t$

Complimentary Counseling Session

Dear Teachers & Students,

We thank you for taking a firm step towards improving your Mathematical abilities. The book you have just purchased has been built with hours of dedication and is trusted by thousands of students like you. Yet, we understand that no two students are identical and each one needs personalized attention.

As a token of our appreciation for your support, **we would like to offer you a free 30 minute counseling session with the author - Savita Maheshwari**. This session is designed to help you understand how to effectively use this workbook and improve your test score. Please reach out to info@smartmathtutoring.com to schedule your free session (Mention subject as "Complimentary Counseling Session").

We always welcome any feedback, suggestions or queries through email to info@smartmathtutoring.com.

With Best Wishes

Smart Math Tutoring

Table of Contents

Complimentary Counseling Session with Author

SECTION 1

NUMBERS, OPERATIONS AND

QUANTITATIVE REASONING

1. Kareena uses a camera to take photographs for a magazine and for a newspaper. Last month she took 120 pictures for the magazine and 150 pictures for the newspaper with this camera. Which proportion can be used to determine p, the percentage of the total number of pictures she took for the magazine?

   A. $\dfrac{p}{100} = \dfrac{150}{270}$

   B. $\dfrac{p}{100} = \dfrac{120}{150}$

   C. $\dfrac{p}{100} = \dfrac{120}{270}$

   D. $\dfrac{p}{100} = \dfrac{270}{120}$

2. During one month, four saplings at a nursery increased in height at the rates shown below.

$$6\%, \frac{1}{12}, 15\%, \frac{1}{18}$$

   Which list shows these rates in order from greatest to least?

   A. $\dfrac{1}{18}, 15\%, \dfrac{1}{12}, 6\%$

   B. $15\%, \dfrac{1}{12}, 6\%, \dfrac{1}{18}$

   C. $\dfrac{1}{18}, 6\%, \dfrac{1}{12}, 15\%$

   D. $15\%, 6\%, \dfrac{1}{12}, \dfrac{1}{18}$

3.	A community center is collecting blankets. The director of the center has asked 145 families to donate 3 blankets each. If 30% to 40% of the families donate 3 blankets each, which of the following could be the number of blankets the center will collect from these families?
	A.	240
	B.	50
	C.	110
	D.	160

4.	As part of a survey, 50 students were asked about their favorite lunch item. The results are shown in the table below.

Favorite Item	Number of Students
Pizza	5
Hamburger	20
Tacos	15
Hot dogs	10

The cafeteria manager knows that about 300 students buy lunch from the cafeteria every day. Based on the table, she predicts that 120 students will buy Hamburger every day. Which statement about her prediction is true?

	A.	Her prediction is invalid because $\frac{1}{5}$ of 50 is 10.
	B.	Her prediction is invalid because $\frac{1}{4}$ of 300 is 75.
	C.	Her prediction is valid because 140% of 50 is 70.
	D.	Her prediction is valid because 40% of 300 is 120.

5. In order to prepare 5 glasses of lemonade juice, Joy uses $\frac{1}{2}$ cups of lemon juice, and $7\frac{1}{2}$ cups of water. If Joy wishes to prepare 12 glasses of lemonade, which proportion can he use to determine how many cups of water, 'w', will he need?

A. $\frac{7.5}{5} = \frac{12}{w}$

B. $\frac{5}{7.5} = \frac{12}{w}$

C. $\frac{12}{5.5} = \frac{5}{w}$

D. $\frac{5}{5.5} = \frac{12}{w}$

6. Mr. Simpson has 4 storage boxes. He is placing 15 lunches in each storage box. Each lunch contains a burger, a bag of nachos, and a shake. About 40 % of these lunches contain a chicken burger. Which of the following is closest to the number of lunches that contain a chicken burger?

A. 24

B. 9

C. 36

D. 8

7. Mike had 42 tickets for games at a carnival. He used $\frac{1}{7}$ of the tickets to play the ball-toss game. He then used $\frac{1}{3}$ of the remaining tickets to play the ring-toss game, in which he won 8 more tickets. How many tickets did Mike have after playing these games?

A. 12

B. 20

C. 32

D. 36

8. There are four students working on an assignment in a class. Mike has completed $\frac{1}{8}$ of the assignment, Emily has completed 10% of the assignment, Gorge has completed 0.13 of the assignment, and Tai has completed $\frac{1}{11}$ of the assignment. Which of the following lists the students in order from greatest to least by the amount of the assignment they completed?
    A. Emily, Mike, Gorge, Tai
    B. Gorge, Mike, Emily, Tai
    C. Emily, Gorge, Mike, Tai
    D. Tai, Emily, Mike, Gorge

9. A mechanic earns $120.00 for 8 hours of work. Which of the following is an equivalent rate?
    A. $120.50 for $6\frac{1}{2}$ hours of work

    B. $127.50 for $8\frac{1}{2}$ hours of work

    C. $178.50 for $7\frac{1}{2}$ hours of work

    D. $153.50 for $9\frac{1}{2}$ hours of work

10. A Gaming parlor charges $18.25 a day for 6 video games. At this rate, which expression can be used to determine the charge for 8 video games for 1 day at this Gaming parlor?
    A. $\frac{18.25}{6}X(8)$

    B. $\frac{6}{18.25}X(8)$

    C. $\frac{23.70}{6}X(8)$

    D. $\frac{6}{23.70}X(8)$

11. The Natrona High School Sports department ordered 500 goodies with the school's mascot printed on them. Out of these goodies, 128 were returned to the printing company because the wrong mascot was printed on them. What percent of the original order did the athletic department keep?
    A. 82%
    B. 37%
    C. 74.4%
    D. 25.6%

12. Wendy read an article which stated an average 16% of men and 11% of women are left-handed. Wendy gathered her own data by surveying adults at a basketball game. She found that 12 out of 32 women were left-handed. What is the difference in percentage between the study's findings and Wendy's experimental results?
    A. 7.2%
    B. 6.3%
    C. 26.5%
    D. 37.5%

13. For her science experiment, Katie chose a magnet that is greater than $\frac{6}{10}$ inch and less than $\frac{12}{18}$ inch. Which of the following could be the length of the magnet she chose?
    A. 0.46 in.
    B. 0.59 in.
    C. 0.64 in.
    D. 0.74 in.

14. Which set of number is in order from least to greatest?

A. $0.004, 4\%, \dfrac{4}{10}, 4, 10^3$

B. $4, \dfrac{4}{10}, 0.004, 10^3, 4\%$

C. $\dfrac{4}{10}, 4\%, 0.004, 4, 10^3$

D. $4, 10^3, 4\%, 0.004, \dfrac{4}{10}$

15. Which numbers are negative integers?

$-\dfrac{3}{4}, 13, -19, 6.05, -3.7, 0, -1$

A. $-\dfrac{3}{4}, -19, -3.7, -1$

B. $13, -19, 0, -1,$

C. $-19, 0, -1$

D. $-19, -1$

16. Which best describes the value of $(5.5)^2$?

A. Greater than 8 and less than 12

B. Greater than 12 and less than 28

C. Greater than 28 and less than 35

D. Greater than 35

17. Hillary was practicing her free throws out of which $\dfrac{2}{5}$ to $\dfrac{3}{5}$ shots hits the target. Which percentage has an equivalent fraction value between $\dfrac{2}{5}$ and $\dfrac{3}{5}$?

A. 8.5%

B. 15%

C. 55%

D. 80%

18. Which of the following is a true statement?

    A. $\frac{4}{5} < 0.60 < 6\%$

    B. $\frac{4}{5} = 0.06 = 6\%$

    C. $\frac{4}{5} > 0.60 = 60\%$

    D. $\frac{4}{5} = 0.60 = 60\%$

19. Annabel is making an egg casserole for breakfast. The recipe makes enough to serve 10 people. How many cups of onion will Annabel need if she wants to prepare enough casserole to serve 5 people?

    A. 1 cup

    B. $\frac{1}{2}$ cup

    C. $\frac{1}{4}$ cup

    D. $\frac{1}{5}$ cup

    Egg Casserole Recipe
    24 eggs
    1 cup sour cream
    1 cup green pepper
    $\frac{1}{2}$ cup onion
    1 teaspoon salt
    1 teaspoon pepper

20. Of the 23 million residents in Texas, about 35% are under the age of 20. About how many Texas residents are under the age of 20?

    A. 6,900,000

    B. 8,050,000

    C. 5,000,000

    D. 6,000,000

21. If $6^{-1} = \frac{1}{6}$ and $6^{-2} = \frac{1}{36}$, what is the value of 6^{-4}?

   A. $\frac{1}{1296}$

   B. $\frac{1}{216}$

   C. $\frac{1}{180}$

   D. 1296

22. Kate, Malcolm, and Guillermo had a competition to find out who could maintain their balance on a beam for the longest amount of time. Malcolm maintained his balance on the beam twice as long as Kate. Guillermo sustained his balance on the beam for 60 seconds, which was $\frac{1}{2}$ as long as Kate. How long did Malcolm retain his balance on the beam?

   A. 1 minute

   B. 2 minute

   C. 3 Minutes

   D. 4 minutes

23. A taxi charges $5 per mile. If the total charge for a cab ride was $14.90, how far was the ride?

   A. 1.98 mi

   B. 2.98 mi

   C. 3.02 mi

   D. 4.02 mi

24. A kilometer is about $\frac{6}{10}$ of a mile. If the speed limit on a stretch of highway in USA is 85 kilometers per hour, what is the approximate speed limit in miles per hour?

   A. 45 mph
   B. 52 mph
   C. 60 mph
   D. 65 mph

25. Geraldo has $13\frac{1}{2}$ pounds of ground sirloin to grill hamburgers for a barbeque. How many quarter-pound hamburgers he can make?

   A. 14
   B. 25
   C. 40
   D. 54

26. Ninth-grade students are offered a selection out of three elective classes for the year. The choices are Band, Choir, and Art. Students may take 1, 2, or 3 of these electives. The Venn diagram shows the relationship among percentages of students who chose to take these electives.

Class Electives

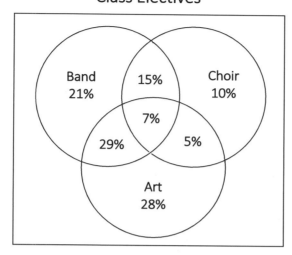

What percentage of ninth-grade students will be taking all three electives?

A. 5%

B. 7%

C. 15%

D. 29%

27. A punch recipe requires 1.5 ounces of juice concentrate to make 9 glasses of punch. According to this recipe, how many glasses of punch can be made from a 12-ounce can of juice concentrate?

A. 72

B. 65

C. 78

D. 62

28. The sun is about 8.7×10^7 miles from the earth. Which of the following numbers represents this distance?
    A. 8,700
    B. 87,000
    C. 8,700,000
    D. 87,000,000

29. A nanometer is equal to 1×10^{-9} meter. Which expression represents this number in standard notation?
    A. 0.0000000001
    B. 0.000000001
    C. 0.0001
    D. 1,000,000,000

30. The workers at a crayon factory can produce an average of 200 crayons every 10 minutes. At this rate, about how long will it take to produce 60,000 crayons?
    A. 50 hours
    B. 41 hours
    C. 55 hours
    D. 35 hours

31. Ms. Nelson constructed a Venn diagram that shows the number of eighth-grade athletes who play volleyball, baseball, and soccer. Which phrase best identifies the number 6 shown in the diagram?

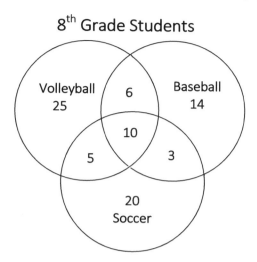

8th Grade Students

A. The total number of athletes who do not play soccer or volleyball.
B. The total number of athletes who play all three sports.
C. The total number of athletes who do not play soccer.
D. The total number of athletes who play both baseball and volleyball, but not soccer.

32. Which of the following rational number is greater than $\frac{1}{14}$ and less than $\frac{1}{12}$?
A. 0.0113
B. 0.0799
C. 0.0186
D. 0.910

33. Aleena is preparing a strawberry dessert for a party. She plans to make 18 servings for every 6 people. If each pan Aleena uses to prepare the dessert holds 4 servings, what is the minimum number of these pans that she needs in order to make enough to feed 18 people?
    A. 14
    B. 16
    C. 13
    D. 54

34. A student had a bottle that contained 64.5 ml of a solution. He used 4.7 ml of the solution for an experiment. Then he poured half the solution remaining in the bottle into a beaker. Finally, he poured 12 ml of the solution remaining in the bottle into a test tube. How many milliliters of solution remained in the bottle?
    A. 23.7 ml
    B. 21.5 ml
    C. 19.15 ml
    D. 17.9 ml

35. A plumber charges $65 for the first hour of labor and $80 for each additional hour of labor. A customer calculates that the plumber charges $265 for a total of $3\frac{1}{2}$ hours of labor. Is the customer correct?
    A. Yes, because 65+ 2.5 x 80 = 540
    B. No, because 80+(65 × 2.5) = 242.50
    C. No, because 65+(80 × 3.5) = 345
    D. Yes, because (80×2.5) + 65 = 265

36. Roland sold candy bars for a school fund-raiser for three weeks. Some information about Roland's candy-bar sales is provided below.
   - Roland sold 28 candy bars during the first week.
   - The number of candy bars he sold during the second week was 6 less than 2 times the number of candy bars he sold during the first week.
   - The number of candy bars he sold during the third week was 8 more than $2\frac{1}{2}$ times the number of candy bars he sold during the second week.

   What was the total number of candy bars Roland sold during the three weeks?
   A. 185
   B. 211
   C. 132
   D. 252

37. Which list shows the numbers below in order from least to greatest?
$$-6\frac{1}{2}, 8.25, \frac{32}{8}, 6\frac{1}{4}, -5.58, \frac{85}{9}$$

   A. $-6\frac{1}{2}, -5.58, \frac{32}{8}, 6\frac{1}{4}, 8.25, \frac{85}{9}$
   B. $-5.58, 6\frac{1}{4}, \frac{32}{8}, -6\frac{1}{2}, \frac{85}{9}, 8.25$
   C. $-6\frac{1}{2}, 6\frac{1}{4}, -5.58, \frac{32}{8}, 8.25, \frac{85}{9}$
   D. $-5.58, -6\frac{1}{2}, 6\frac{1}{4}, \frac{32}{8}, 8.25, \frac{85}{9}$

38. A baseball coach bought some bats and gloves for the school's baseball team. The bats cost $28 to $36, and the gloves cost $40 to $60. Which of the following does NOT represent a reasonable total purchase price for 16 bats and 12 gloves?
   A. $1,480
   B. $980
   C. $1,200
   D. $1,130

39. One weekend Sam and Daniel worked in McDonalds to earn spending money. Together they earned $12.50 an hour for 9 hours of work. Each received half of the total earnings. If Sam then spent $15 on a new CD, what was the total amount he had left, in dollars and cents, from the money he earned working that weekend?

40. Which numbers from this list are less than −0.84?

$$-\frac{14}{16}, -0.24, -2.23, 97\%, -3\frac{2}{5}, -0.94$$

A. $-\frac{14}{16}, -2.23,$ and -0.94

B. $-\frac{14}{16}, -3\frac{2}{5}, -2.23,$ and -0.94

C. $-0.24, -\frac{14}{16},$ and $-0.94, -2.23$

D. $-\frac{14}{16}, 0.24,$ and -2.23

41. An electrician charges $65 for the first hour of labor and $50 for each additional hour of labor. A customer calculates that the electrician charges $'c' for a total of $2\frac{1}{2}$ hours of labor. Is the customer correct?

A. Yes, because (65×2.5) −50= c

B. No, because 50+(65 × 2.5) = c

C. Yes, because 65+(50 × 1.5) = c

D. No, because (65×2.5) −50= c

42. A store sells a 6-pound bag of apples for $5.60. Which of the following is NOT an equivalent price per pound of apples?

A. A 30-pound bag for $28.03

B. A 12-pound bag for $10.80

C. A 7-pound bag for 6.54 $

D. A15-pound bag for $14.01

43.   Oksona spends from $30 to $40 at the grocery store each week. She spends about 30% of the amount on vegetables and fruit. Which of the following is a reasonable estimate of the amount of money Oksona will spend on vegetables and fruit at the grocery store during the next 4 weeks?
    A. $120
    B. $30
    C. $45
    D. $24

44.   The average distance from Earth to the sun is about 9.4×10^7 miles. The average distance from Mars to the sun is about 1.6×10^8 miles. When both planets are at their average distance from the sun, how much further is Mars from the sun than Earth?
    A. 66,000,000 mi
    B. 57,000,000 mi
    C. 107,000,000 mi
    D. 233,000,000 mi

45. The water levels of five Texas lakes were measured on the same day in 2010. The table below shows the number of feet above or below normal level for each lake

Water level of Taxes Lakes

Lake	Number of Feet Above or Below Normal Level
Travis	0.12
Possum Kingdom	-2.56
Richland Chambers	0.16
Amistad	-1.52
Conroe	0.07

Which list shows the numbers in the table from greatest to least?
A. −25.6, −1.52, 0.16, 0.12, 0.07
B. 0.16, 0.12, 0.07, −1.52, −2.56
C. 0.16, 0.12, 0.07, −2.56, −1.52
D. −2.56, −1.52, 0.07, 0.12, 0.16

46. Harry places a rubber duck in the current of the Rio Grande River. The rubber duck floats 13 miles downstream in $3\frac{2}{5}$ hours. At this rate, about how many miles will the duck travel in 5 hours?
A. 15 miles
B. 20 miles
C. 27 miles
D. 30 miles

47. Lorenzo was in the Tower of the Americas in San Antonio, Texas. He dropped a ball from an open window 60 feet above the ground. If the ball rebounds half the distance, it drops each time it bounces, what will be the height of the rebound after the fourth bounce?
A. 3.75 ft
B. 7.5 ft
C. 15 ft
D. 30 ft

48. During a field trip to a park, Mr. Hamilton's Earth Science class collected rocks. There were 14 boys and 16 girls in his class. The least number of rocks collected by a student was 18, and the greatest number was 34. Which is a reasonable total number of rocks collected by all the students?
A. 540
B. 476
C. 728
D. 980

49. The total population of San Francisco is about 23,600,000. What is this number in scientific notation?
A. 2.36×10^{-7}
B. 2.36×10^{-6}
C. 2.36×10^{6}
D. 2.36×10^{7}

50.   The state of Ohio has 80 counties. Texas has 14 fewer than 3 ½ times as many counties. How many counties are in Texas?
   A. 266
   B. 224
   C. 244
   D. 39

51.   Bacteria grown in a lab double in population every 30 minutes. If 80 bacteria are in a Sandy dish at 3:00 P.M., how many bacteria will be in the Sandy dish at 5:00 P.M.?
   A. 160
   B. 320
   C. 640
   D. 1280

52.   Between which two whole numbers is $\sqrt{85}$?
   A. 10 and 11
   B. 9 and 10
   C. 8 and 9
   D. 7 and 8

53.   Mr. McMillan writes four irrational numbers on the board and asks one of his eighth grade students to choose the number that is closest to her age. Which of these irrational numbers did the student most likely choose?
   A. π
   B. $\sqrt{23}$
   C. $\sqrt{190}$
   D. $\sqrt{1398}$

54. A hydrogen molecule is 1.9 angstrom in length. What is this number in standard notation? If 1m = 10,000,000,000 angstrom.
    A. 0.000000019 meter
    B. 0.0000000019 meter
    C. 0.00000000019 meter
    D. 0.000000000019 meter

55. People have about 23,000,000,000,000 red blood cells in their bodies at any given time. What is this number in scientific notation?
    A. 2.3×10^{10}
    B. 2.3×10^{11}
    C. 2.3×10^{12}
    D. 2.3×10^{13}

56. The diameter of mercury is 5,203 miles. What is this number in scientific notation?
    A. 5.203×10^{-4}
    B. 5.203×10^{-3}
    C. 5.203×10^{3}
    D. 5.203×10^{4}

57. Light travels at approximately 1.325×10^{6} km per hour. What is this speed in standard notation?
    A. 1,325 kmph
    B. 3,250 kmph
    C. 132,500 kmph
    D. 1,325,000 kmph

58. One light year is approximately 5.894×10^{12} miles. What is this number in standard notation?
   A. 5.894 million miles
   B. 5,894,000 miles
   C. 5,894,000,000 miles
   D. 5,894,000,000,000 miles

59. What is the area of the largest square in the figure below?

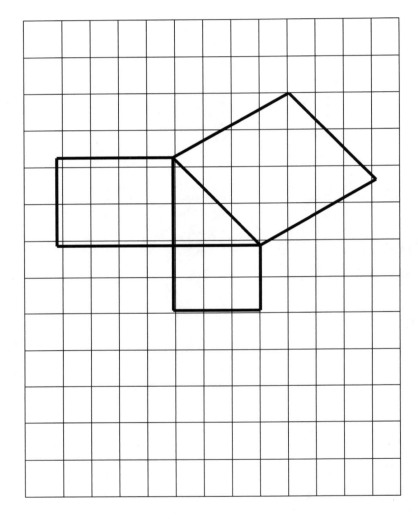

   A. 5 square units
   B. 34 square units
   C. 16 square units
   D. 25 square units

60.   A large Oak tree in Mrs. Charlie's yard was struck by lightning and fell as shown in the diagram below. What was the total height of the tree before it falls?

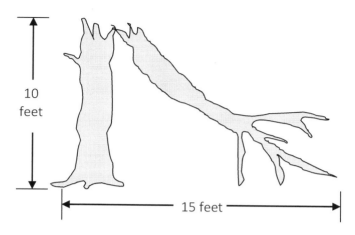

A. 25 ft
B. 18 ft
C. 28 ft
D. 15 ft

61.   Cora bought 4 oranges priced at $0.31 each and 2 loaves of bread priced at $1.50 each. There was no sales tax on these items. She gave the cashier $5.00. How much change did she receive?
A. $4.24
B. $1.24
C. $0.76
D. $3.00

62.   When 9 is added to the product of 7 and another number, the result is 65. What is the other number?
A. -15
B. 8
C. 10.6
D. 14

63.　In a number game, Troy was supposed to find the square root of a number. Instead, he squared the number and wrote 36. What number was he supposed to write?

A. 3

B. 1.8

C. 6

D. 2.4

64.　Which subset of the real number contains $\sqrt{5}$?

A. Irrational number

B. Rational numbers

C. Integers

D. Whole numbers

65.   Which point on following number line shows $x = -\sqrt{18}$?

A.

B.

C.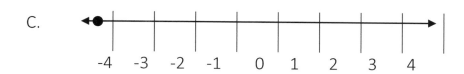

D.

66. Which of the following sets is represented by the Venn diagram below?

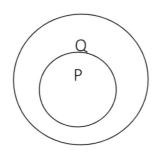

A. Set P = odd integers
   Set Q = even integers
B. Set P = rational numbers
   Set Q = irrational numbers
C. Set P = integers
   Set Q = rational numbers
D. Set P = rational numbers
   Set Q = integers

67. The area of the state of L.A. is about 7.987×10^5 square kilometers. How can you write this number in standard notation?
   A. 79,870
   B. 798,700
   C. 7,987,000
   B. 79,870,000

68. The total area of the state of Texas is about 3,890,000 square miles. What is this number expressed in scientific notation?
   A. 3.89×10^{-6}
   B. 3.89×10^{-5}
   C. 3.89×10^5
   D. 3.89×10^6

69. Four students are each trying to raise the same amount of money for a class trip. The table below shows how much of each student's goal has been met.

Fund-Raiser Progress

Student	Part of Goal Met
Charles	0.9
Dmitri	$\frac{2}{3}$
Niang	$\frac{5}{8}$
Marry	85%

Which list shows the numbers in the table in order from least to greatest?
A. 0.9, 85%, $\frac{5}{8}$, $\frac{2}{3}$
B. 0.9, $\frac{5}{8}$, 85%, $\frac{2}{3}$
C. $\frac{5}{8}$, 85%, $\frac{2}{3}$, 0.9
D. $\frac{5}{8}$, $\frac{2}{3}$, 85%, 0.9

70. Samuel used a microscope to measure the diameter of a hair. He found that the diameter of the hair was 0.000076 meter. How is this number written in scientific notation?
A. 7.6×10^{-5}
B. 7.6×10^{6}
C. 7.6×10^{5}
D. 7.6×10^{-6}

71. Three groups of students used different methods to estimate the diagonal length of a patio in feet. Their results were:

- $5\sqrt{13}$ ft
- $15\frac{2}{5}$ ft
- 15.33 ft

Which list shows these diagonal lengths in order from greatest to least?

A. $15.33, 15\frac{2}{5}, 5\sqrt{13}$

B. $15.33, 5\sqrt{13}, 15\frac{2}{5}$

C. $15\frac{2}{5}, 15.33, 5\sqrt{13}$

D. $5\sqrt{13}, 15\frac{2}{5}, 15.33$

72. The areas of squares A and B are shown in the diagram below. What is the area of square C?

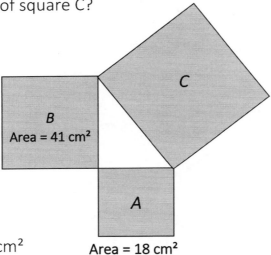

A. 10.6 cm²
B. 23 cm²
C. 59 cm²
D. 2,005 cm²

73.   Which list shows the numbers below in order from least to greatest?

$$5.78, -5.9, 58\%, -\frac{23}{4}$$

A. $-5.9, -\frac{23}{4}, 5.78, 58\%$

B. $-\frac{23}{4}, -5.9, 58\%, 5.78$

C. $-5.9, -\frac{23}{4}, 58\%, 5.78$

D. $58\%, -\frac{23}{4}, 5.78, -5.9$

74.   Two numbers are shown on the number line.

$\frac{\sqrt{9}}{3}$ 2π

Which value is NOT located between these two numbers on the number line?

A. π

B. $\sqrt{9}$

C. $\frac{\pi}{9}$

D. $\frac{\pi^2}{9}$

75. The mass of a comic book is approximately 0.00165 metric ton. How is this number written in scientific notation?
   A. 165×10^{-5}
   B. 1.65×10^{-3}
   C. 16.5×10^{-4}
   D. 0.165×10^{-2}

76. The number of gift baskets Selena can make varies directly with the amount of time she spends making the baskets. She can make 8 baskets in $\frac{1}{2}$ hour. How many baskets can Selena make in 7 hours?

77. A can of fruit drink contains 225 calories per 2.5 servings. Which of the following is NOT an equivalent number of calories per serving?
   A. 360 calories per 4 servings
   B. 1,170 calories per 13 servings
   C. 750 calories per 8 servings
   D. 810 calories per 9 servings

78. Which point on the number line best represents the location of $\sqrt{92}$?

   A. Point M
   B. Point N
   C. Point P
   D. Point Q

79.   The drawing below shows a side view of a picture frame on Naira's desk.

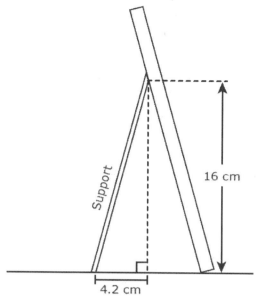

Which of the following is closest to the length of the frame support?
A. 20 cm
B. 15 cm
C. 12 cm
D. 17 cm

80. Daniel placed a 14-feet ladder against the side of his house so that the base of the ladder was 5 feet away from the base of the house, as shown in the diagram below.

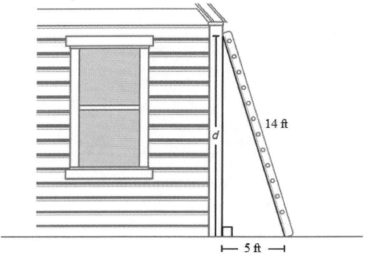

Which measurement in feet is closest to *d*, the distance from the top of the ladder to the ground?
A. 13.1 ft
B. 14.8 ft
C. 16.5 ft
D. 19.6ft

81.   A side view of a desk telephone is shown below.

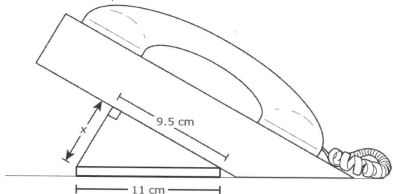

Which of the following is closest to the value of x?

A. 2 cm

B. 10 cm

C. 20 cm

D. 6 cm

82.   A 10-foot ladder is leaning against a wall. The bottom of the ladder is 4 feet away from the base of the wall.

Which of the following is closest to the distance from the top of the ladder to the base of the wall?

A. 9 ft

B. 11 ft

C. 6 ft

D. 14 ft

83. Which group of three squares will form a right triangle when joined at their vertices?

A.

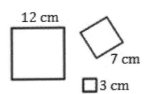

B.

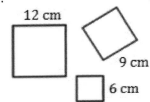

C.

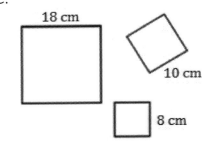

D.

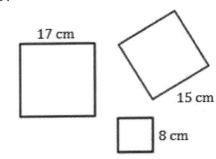

84. Calvin filed his flight plan for a trip in his single-engine plane. He took off towards east from the airport. He flew in east for 50 miles, made a 90 degree turn, and flew south for 120 miles. At this point how far, in a direct line, was Calvin from the airport?

A. 75 miles

B. 100 miles

C. 130 miles

D. 190 miles

85. In the diagram below, *RSTU* is a rectangle, and the two shaded regions are squares.

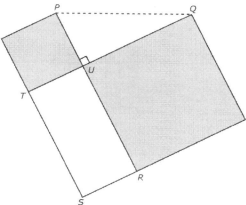

If the length of $\overline{SR}$ is 5 m and the length of $\overline{ST}$ is 9 m, what is the length of $\overline{PQ}$ in meters?

A. $\sqrt{80}$ m

B. $\sqrt{106}$ m

C. $\sqrt{68}$ m

D. $\sqrt{144}$ m

86. The change in water level of a lake is shown in the table below. How much did the water level change between Weeks 2 and 3?

Week	1	2	3	4
Water Level (inches)	$1\frac{3}{8}$	$-2\frac{1}{4}$	$1\frac{5}{8}$	$-1\frac{1}{2}$

A. $\frac{1}{2}$

B. $\frac{5}{8}$

C. $3\frac{3}{4}$

D. $3\frac{7}{8}$

87. What is the longest stick that can be placed inside a box with inside dimensions of 55 inches, 75 inches, and 45 inches? Round the answer to the nearest hundredth.

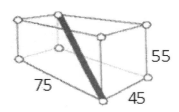

88. What is the longest stick that can be placed inside a box with inside dimensions of 60 inches, 30 inches, and 30 inches? Round the answer to the nearest tenth.

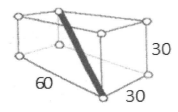

89. Which number is a rational number, but not an integer?
    A. $-\sqrt{144}$
    B. $-\sqrt{\dfrac{218}{12}}$
    C. $\sqrt{\dfrac{196}{4}}$
    D. 99

90. Which statement is false?
    A. All rational numbers are real numbers.
    B. All irrational numbers are real numbers.
    C. All integers are rational numbers.
    D. All irrational numbers are rational numbers.

91. Which number line shows the best approximation of $\sqrt{99}$?

A.

B.

C.

D.

92. Which of the following number sets can be represented by the Venn diagram below?

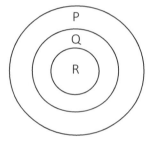

A. Set P = 0, 2, 4, 6
   Set Q = 1, 3, 5, 7
   Set R = 1.5, 3.7, 2.2

B. Set P = -8, -6, 9, 12
   Set Q = 3.1, -5, 6, 10.1
   Set R = 1, 4, 8, 12

C. Set P = -8, -2, 6, 9
   Set Q = 0, 2, 4, 5
   Set R = 1, 2, 3, 5

D. Set P = 4, 9, 15, 23
   Set Q = 0, 2, 3, 5
   Set R = -3, -2, 0, 1

93.   Following graph shows motion of a car. It can be described as:

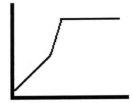

A. The car drove at a constant speed and stopped.
B. The car is traveling at constant speed.
C. The car drove at a constant speed, then stopped, then drove at a constant speed again.
D. The car drove at constant speed, then increased its speed and then stopped.

94.   Which numbers can belong to following circles?

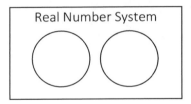

A. 3.6, 5
B. $\sqrt{14}$, 6.5
C. -8, -9
D. None

95. Following graphs shows different motions of a car. Which graph shows that a car drove at a constant speed and stopped?

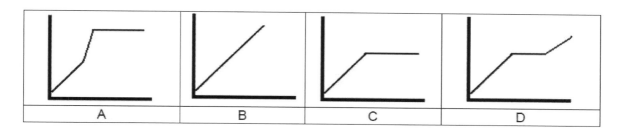

Answer Key

		Marks (C/W)
1	C	
2	B	
3	D	
4	D	
5	B	
6	A	
7	C	
8	B	
9	B	
10	A	
11	C	
12	C	
13	C	
14	A	
15	D	
16	C	
17	C	
18	C	
19	C	
20	B	
21	A	
22	D	
23	B	
24	B	
25	D	
26	B	
27	A	
28	D	
29	B	
30	A	
31	D	
32	B	
	Total	

		Marks (C/W)
33	A	
34	D	
35	D	
36	B	
37	A	
38	A	
39	$41.25	
40	B	
41	C	
42	B	
43	C	
44	A	
45	B	
46	B	
47	A	
48	C	
49	D	
50	A	
51	D	
52	B	
53	C	
54	C	
55	D	
56	C	
57	D	
58	D	
59	B	
60	C	
61	C	
62	B	
63	D	
64	A	
	Total	

		Marks (C/W)
65	C	
66	C	
67	B	
68	D	
69	D	
70	A	
71	D	
72	C	
73	C	
74	C	
75	B	
76	112	
77	C	
78	C	
79	D	
80	A	
81	D	
82	A	
83	D	
84	C	
85	B	
86	D	
87	103.32	
88	73.5	
89	B	
90	D	
91	C	
92	C	
93	D	
94	B	
95	C	
96		
	Total	

SECTION 2

PATTERNS, RELATIONSHIPS AND

ALGEBRAIC REASONING

1. Billy has a collection of postage stamps from different countries. He has one book that contains 38 stamps. He has a second book that has 8 stamps on each page. The equation below can be used to find x, the total number of postage stamps Billy has if the second book has y pages.

$$x = 38 + 8y$$

How many postage stamps does Billy have in all if the second book has 15 pages?

2. The graph models the value of a lathe machine over a 10-year period.

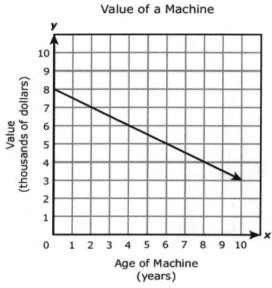

Which equation best represents the relationship between t, the age of the lathe machine in years, and p, the value of the machine in dollars over this 10-year period?

A. $p = -0.002t + 2{,}500$

B. $p = -500t + 8{,}000$

C. $p = 500t + 8{,}000$

D. $p = 0.002t + 2{,}500$

3. Mark had p tickets for the rides at Auto expo. . He kept 10 of the tickets and gave an equal number of the remaining tickets to 7 of his friends. There were no tickets left over. Which equation can be used to find f, the number of tickets Mark gave to each of his friends?

A. $f = \frac{p}{7} + 10$

B. $f = \frac{p+10}{7}$

C. $f = \frac{p}{7} - 10$

D. $f = \frac{p-10}{7}$

4. Sebastian is getting a new deck built. He paid $485 for the required materials, and he will pay his brother $25 an hour to build the deck. Which table shows the relationship between h, the number of hours Sebastian's brother works, and c, the total cost of the project?

A.

h	c
0	485
3	510
8	535
12	560

C.

h	c
0	485
3	560
8	685
12	785

B.

h	c
0	510
3	535
8	560
12	585

D.

h	c
0	510
3	585
8	710
12	810

5. A company conducts research to predict how a new advertisement affects the sales of a product. The equation below can be used to determine n, the number of people who will buy the product if r people read the advertisement.

$$n = 0.6r + 368$$

If 500 people bought the product last week, how many people read the advertisement?

A. 186
B. 220
C. 1,200
D. 3,700

6. Fernandez is walking 10,000 feet for a fund-raiser. He walks at a rate of 270 feet per minute. This situation is modeled by the equation below, where d represents the remaining number of feet Fernandez has to walk and t represents the number of minutes he has already walked.

$$d=10,000-270t$$

Which table shows the only values that satisfy this equation?

A.

t	d
1	9,730
3	9,190
8	7,840
10	7,300

C.

t	d
1	10,000
3	9,460
8	8,110
10	7,570

B.

t	d
1	9,730
3	9,460
8	9,190
10	8,920

D.

t	d
1	10,000
3	9,730
8	9,640
10	9,190

7. Which equation best describes a relationship between x and *y* in the table below?

X	Y
0	3
6	5
12	7

A. y = 3x + 5

B. $y = \frac{1}{3}x + 3$

C. $y = \frac{1}{4}x + 3$

D. y = x + 5

8. A 12-inch candle burns at a rate of 4 inches an hour. Which equation represents the relationship between *h*, the height of the candle in inches, and *b*, the number of hours the candle burns?

A. h = 4*b* + 9

B. $h = 12 - 4b$

C. $h = 4 - 12b$

D. $h = 12b + 4$

9. Ms. Jennifer spends $95 each month dining out at fast food restaurants. She plans to reduce her spending for fast food by $7each month until she has reduced her spending to $35 per month. Which equation can be used to determine m, the number of months it will take for Ms. Jennifer to reduce her fast food spending to $35 per month?

A. $\frac{1}{3}(7m + 95) = 35$

B. 95 - 7m = 35

C. 7m + 95m = 35

D. $\frac{1}{3}m + 95 = 35$

10. Jack mown lawns to earn money. He buys a new mower for $215 and charges $50 per lawn. If he mows n lawns, which of the following equations could you use to find p, Jack's profit?
    A. p = 50n - 215
    B. p = 50n + 215
    C. p = n (215 – 50)
    D. p = 215 – 50n

11. Serena and Venus are playing a game in which the aim is to be the first to reach the finishing line. They start the game by standing 30 feet away from the finishing line. Venus always move one half the distance between herself and the finishing line. Serena always moves 1.5 feet toward the finishing line. Who will reach the finish line first?
    A. It will be a tie.
    B. No one will win.
    C. Venus
    D. Serena

12. Ciara has $15 more than Maggie. Together they have $46. Which equation could be solved to find *m*, the amount Maggie has?
    A. (m – 15) + m = 46
    B. m + (m + 15) = 46
    C. m = 25 – 46
    D. m = (25 + m) – 46

13. Roddick attained an average score of 85.5 on his first two math tests. He earned a score of 92 on his third test. Which equation can be used to find x, Roddick's average math test score for the three tests?

A. $x = \dfrac{85.5 + 92}{3}$

B. $x = \dfrac{(85.5 \div 2) + 92}{3}$

C. $x = \dfrac{(85.5 \times 2) + 92}{3}$

D. $x = \dfrac{85.5}{3} \times 2$

14. What is the value of $\dfrac{n^2}{7} + n - 22$ if n = -7?

A. -46

B. 34

C. -22

D. 38

15. A cotton milling company employs 450 workers. The management plans to increase the workforce by 16 employees per week until they have tripled the workforce size. Which equation can be used to determine w, the number of weeks it will require for the company's workforce to triple in size?

A. 16w = 1,350 + 450

B. 16 + 450 w = 1,350

C. 16w + 450 = 1,350

D. 3(16w + 450) = 450

16. Wayne swam 100 meters in 2 minutes 30 seconds. Kathleen swam 300 meters in 3 minutes. Based on these rates, which statement is true?

   A. Wayne's average speed was 6 meters per minute faster than Kathleen's average speed.
   B. Kathleen's average speed was 60 meters per minute faster than Wayne's average speed.
   C. Kathleen's average speed was 3 meters per second faster than Wayne's average speed.
   D. Wayne's average speed was equal to Kathleen's average speed.

17. The formula used for converting the temperature from Fahrenheit (F) to Celsius (C) is $°C = \frac{5}{9} (°F-32)$. If the temperature in L.A. is 82°F what is the approximate temperature in degrees Celsius?
   A. 176°C
   B. 140° C
   C. 41° C
   D. 27° C

18. Ms. Williams receives commission for selling home security systems. Her commission doubles with each system she sells. How much will her commission be if she sells 7 security systems?

Security Systems Sold	Dollars of Commission
1	$10
2	$20
3	$40
4	$80

A. $320
B. $480
C. $640
D. $720

19. What value of x makes this equation true?

$$0.8x - 7 = 0.4x + 9$$

A. 4
B. 34
C. 24
D. 40

20. Emily's bank charges a $20 checking account fee per month plus a $0.18 fee for every check she writes. The equation below gives c, the total cost of the checking account for a month in which n checks are written.

$$c = 20 + 0.18n$$

How many checks did Emily write during a month in which her total checking account fees was $24.14?

A. 8
B. 23
C. 14
D. 180

21. Which steps could be used to solve the equation?

$$\frac{2}{4}x + 9 = 17$$

A. Subtract 9 from both sides, then divide both sides by the reciprocal of $\frac{2}{4}$.

B. Subtract 9 from both sides, then multiply both sides by the reciprocal of $\frac{2}{4}$.

C. Multiply both sides by the reciprocal of $\frac{2}{4}$, then subtract 9 from both sides.

D. Divide both sides by 2, then multiply both sides by 4 and subtract 9.

22. Which of the following equation shows the relationship between x and y in the table?

x	y
-4	-14
-1	-5
0	-2
2	4
9	25

A. y = 3x − 2

B. y = -4x

C. y = x²

D. y = 3x

23. Let n represent the position of a number in the following sequence.

$$\frac{1}{2}, 1, \frac{3}{2}, 2 \ldots$$

Which expression can be used to find any term in the sequence?

A. $2n$

B. $\frac{1}{2}n$

C. $\frac{3}{2}n$

D. $n + \frac{1}{2}$

24. The following formula can be used to determine the recommended maximum pulse rate during an exercise for people of different ages.

$$P = \frac{4(200 - X)}{5}$$

The person's age in years is X, and the maximum pulse rate in pulse per minute is P. If Kelly's pulse is monitored 140 pulse/min then how old should she be?

A. 28

B. 35

C. 25

D. Not here

25. David sells video games on a web site. The cost for his web site is $65 per year. David sells each video game for $35. Which equation can David use to determine how many video games 'g', he must sell to make a profit of $50 per year?

A. 100g = 50

B. 65 - 35g = 50

C. 35g + 65 = 50

D. 35g – 65 = 50

26. The table shows the relationship between the number of cupcakes k, and the total cost c, in dollars for an order of cupcakes.

Number of Cupcakes, k	Cost in Dollars, c
1	$0.40
2	$0.55
3	$0.70
4	$0.85
5	$1.00
6	$1.15

Which equation shows the total cost for an order of cupcakes?
A. $c = 0.15\,k + 0.25$
B. $c = 0.25\,k + 0.15$
C. $c = 0.25\,k$
D. $c = 0.40\,k$

27. The equation c = 10 + .06m represents Quinn's monthly cell phone cost c, in dollars for m minutes of peak usage time. Which table reflects this equation?

A.

Monthly Cell Phone Cost

m	100	200	300	400
c	16	22	28	34

B.

Monthly Cell Phone Cost

m	10	20	30	40
c	6	12	18	24

C.

Monthly Cell Phone Cost

m	1	2	3	4
c	16	22	28	34

D.

Monthly Cell Phone Cost

m	1000	2000	3000	4000
c	16	22	28	34

28. The table below shows attendance at the library for preschool story time for the first four weeks of the year. Which of the following equations describes the data?

Week (w)	Number of Children (c)
1	40
2	50
3	60
4	70

A. $c = 10w + 30$

B. $c = 30w + 10$

C. $c = 40w$

D. $c = 30w$

29. A root beer stand sells glasses of root beer in 4 different sizes. Jimmie and his friends bought 2 small drinks for $1.39 each, 2 medium drinks for $1.50 each, and 4 large drinks for $1.59 each. Which equation can be used to find a, the average price they paid for a glass of root beer?

A. $a = \dfrac{(2 \times 1.39)+(2 \times 1.50)+(4 \times 1.59)}{7}$

B. $a = \dfrac{1.39 + 1.50 + 1.59}{3}$

C. $a = \dfrac{1.39 \times 1.50 \times 1.59}{7}$

D. $a = \dfrac{(2 \times 1.39) + (2 \times 1.50) +(4 \times 1.59)}{8}$

30. Laura can type 80 words per minute. Which of the following represents typing at the same rate?

A. 35 words in 30 seconds

B. 40 words in 50 seconds

C. 60 words in 45 seconds

D. 75 words in 55 seconds

31. Renting video games from Store S costs $3.50 per game plus a monthly fee of $7.00. Renting video games from Store T costs $7.00 per game with no monthly fee. The monthly cost to rent video games depends on the number of video games, v, rented. Which inequality represents the situation when the monthly cost at Store S is less than the monthly cost at Store T?

   A. $3.5v + 7 < 7v$

   B. $3.5v + 7 > 7v$

   C. $10.5v < 7v$

   D. $10.5v > 7v$

32. What is the value of the function $g(n) = \frac{1}{6}(n - 30)$ when $n = 114$?

   A. 4

   B. 9

   C. 14

   D. 16

33. The table shows the pattern of a sequence. Which expression describes the pattern?

n	s
1	1
2	1.5
3	2
4	2.5

   A. $\frac{n}{2}$

   B. $\frac{n}{2} - 1$

   C. $\frac{n+1}{2}$

   D. $\frac{2n-3}{2}$

34. The value of y varies directly with x. When y = 75, $x = \frac{1}{2}$. What is the value of y when x is $2\frac{1}{4}$?

A. $84\frac{3}{8}$

B. $337\frac{1}{2}$

C. $16\frac{2}{3}$

D. $168\frac{3}{4}$

35. Which table contains only corresponding x-values and y-values where the value of y is 3 more than the quotient of x and 2?

F

x	y
7	5
10	6.5
14	8.5
17	10

H

x	y
7	3.5
10	5
14	7
17	8.5

G

x	y
7	6.5
10	8
14	10
17	11.5

J

x	y
7	0.5
10	2
14	4
17	5.5

36.   The model represents an equation.

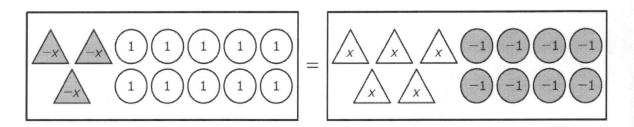

What value of x makes the equation true?

37.   The graph models the linear relationship between the charge for a trip and the number of miles driven by two taxis.

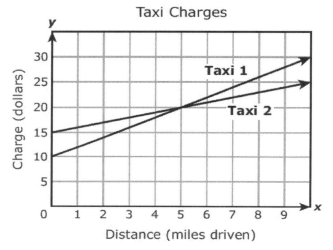

Based on the graph, which statement appears to be true?
A. The charge for a trip with a distance of 5 miles is $5 more for Taxi 1 than for Taxi 2.
B. The charge for a trip with a distance of 5 miles is $5 less for Taxi 1 than for Taxi 2.
C. The charge for a trip with a distance of 5 miles is $20 for both Taxi 1 and Taxi 2.
D. The charge for a trip with a distance of 5 miles cannot be determined for either Taxi 1 or Taxi 2.

38. Senorita is ordering sweatshirts for her school. Company P charges $4.50 for each sweatshirt and a one-time engraving fee of $30. Company R charges $6.50 for each sweatshirt and a one-time engraving fee of $19. Which inequality can be used to find x, the minimum number of sweatshirts that can be ordered, so that the total charges by Company P is less than the total charge by Company R?

    A. $4.50 + 30x < 6.50 + 19x$
    B. $4.50 + 30x > 6.50 + 19x$
    C. $4.50x + 30 < 6.50x + 19$
    D. $4.50x + 30 > 6.50x + 19$

39. Which graph represents y as a function of x?

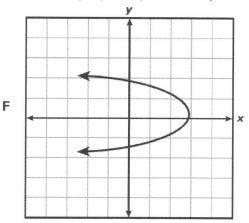

F

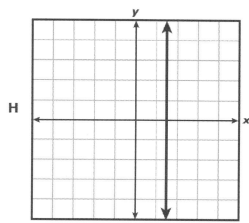

H

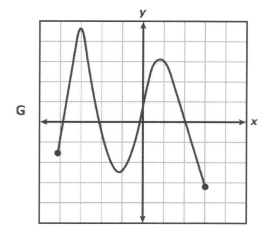

G

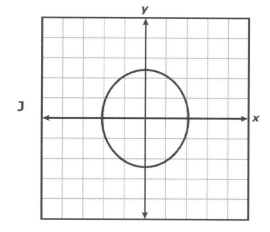

J

40. Which graph best represents the equation y = 2x?

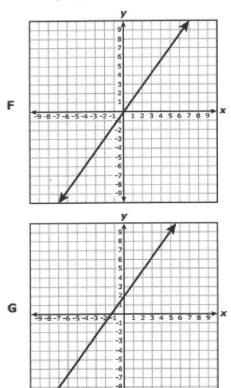

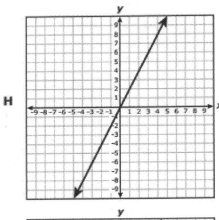

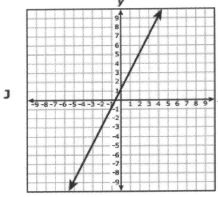

41. Ria sells 6 ice cream cups for $7.50. She sells other ice-cream cups with same unit rate. If you were to graph the line of this proportional relationship between cost of ice cream cups and number of ice cream cups, which of the following pairs of coordinates represent points on the line?

A. (1, 3.50) and (2, 4.50)
B. (2, 2.50) and (10, 12)
C. (10, 12.5) and (15, 18.75)
D. (2, 2.75) and (5, 6.50)

42.   Which function is best represented by this graph with its domain?

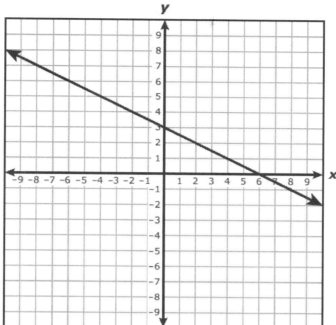

A. $y = \frac{1}{2}x + 3$, D: -9 ≤ x ≤ 9

B. $y = -2x + 3$, D: -2 ≤ x ≤ 8

C. $y = -2x + 6$, D: x is all real numbers

D. $y = -\frac{1}{2}x + 3$, D: x is all real numbers

43. What are the slope and the y-intercept of the graph of the linear function shown on the grid?

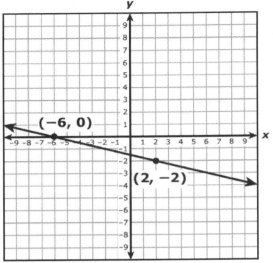

A. Slope = 4, y–intercept = –6

B. Slope = –4, y–intercept = –1.5

C. Slope = $-\frac{1}{4}$, y–intercept = –1.5

D. Slope = $\frac{1}{4}$, y–intercept = – 6

44.   Which graph shows a proportional relationship between x and y?

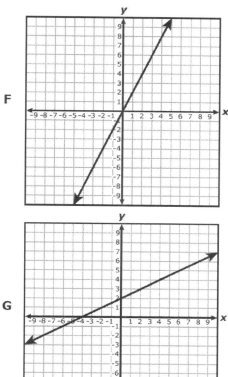

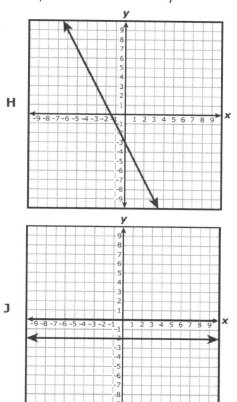

45. Which statement describes the mapping?

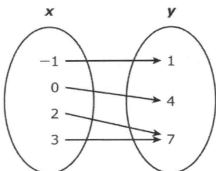

A. The mapping represents y as a function of x, because each y-value corresponds to exactly one x-value.

B. The mapping does not represent y as a function of x, because two of the x-values correspond to the same y-value.

C. The mapping represents y as a function of x, because each x-value corresponds to exactly one y-value.

D. The mapping does not represent y as a function of x, because there are more x-values than different corresponding y-values.

46.   A water hose discharges water at a rate of 45 gallons per minute. Which graph has a slope that best represents this rate?

F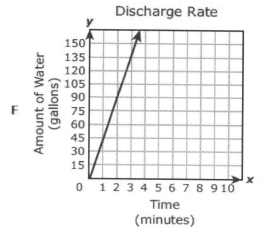

H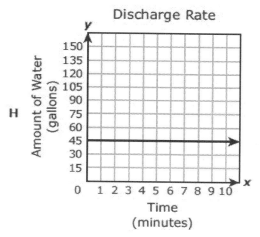

G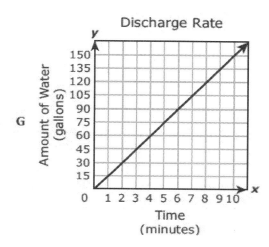

J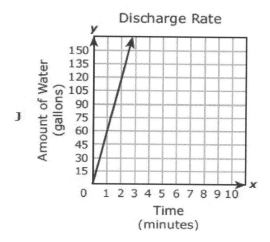

47.   The table shows the number of gallons of gasoline in a car's gas tank after the car has been driven for x miles.

Gasoline Usage

Miles Driven, x	Gallons of Gasoline in the Tank, y
0	15
10	14.6
20	14.2
35	13.6
60	12.6
75	12

When these data are graphed on a coordinate grid, the points all lie on the same line. What are the slope and y-intercept of this line?

A. Slope $= \frac{1}{25}$, y-intercept $= 375$

B. Slope $= -\frac{1}{25}$, y-intercept $= 15$

C. Slope $= 25$, y-intercept $= 375$

D. Slope $= -25$, y-intercept $= 15$

48. The approximate volume in milliliters, m, for a volume of f fluid ounces is equal to 29.57 times the value of f. Which table represents this relationship?

Liquid Volume

A.

Fluid Ounces, f	Milliliters, me
29.57	1
59.14	2
88.71	3
118.28	4

Liquid Volume

C.

Fluid Ounces, f	Milliliters, me
0	29.57
1	59.14
2	88.71
3	118.28

Liquid Volume

B.

Fluid Ounces, f	Milliliters, me
29.57	0
59.14	1
88.71	2
118.28	3

Liquid Volume

D.

Fluid Ounces, f	Milliliters, me
1	29.57
2	59.14
3	88.71
4	118.28

49.   Which graph does NOT represent y as a function of x?

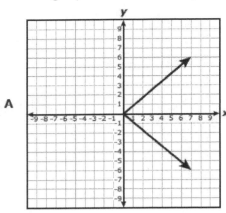

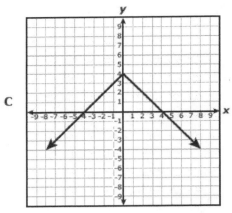

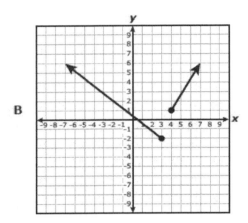

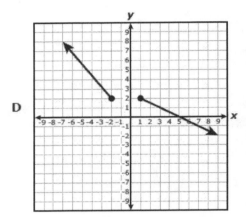

50.   What value of x makes this equation true?

$$\frac{x}{3} - 3 = \frac{x}{9} + 3$$

51. Two eighth-grade classes are selling Art Gallery tickets to raise money.
    - One class is selling tickets for $2.50 each and has already raised $350.
    - The other class is selling tickets for $3.00 each and has already raised $225.

    Which equation can be used to find t, the number of tickets each class needs to sell so that the total amount raised is the same for both classes?

    A. 3t + 350 = 2.50 t + 225

    B. 350t + 2.50 = 225t + 3

    C. 2.50 t + 350 = 3t + 225

    D. Not here

52. The graph shows the relationship between the cost of some pecans and the weight of the pecans in pounds.

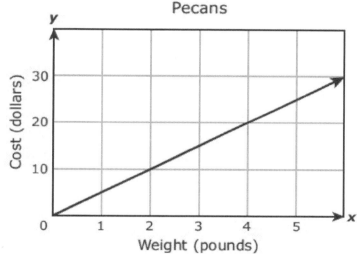

Pecans

Which function best represents the relationship shown in the graph?

A. $y = 5x$

B. $y = \dfrac{1}{5x}$

C. $y = 2x$

D. $y = \dfrac{1}{2x}$

53.   Which graph shows the most steepness?

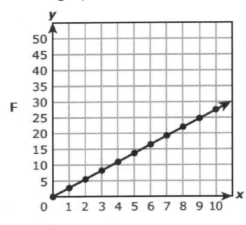

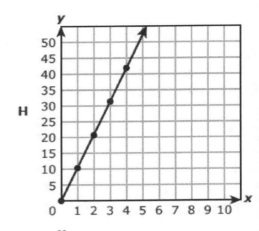

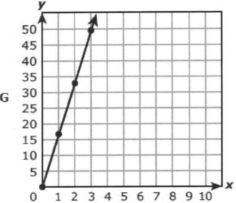

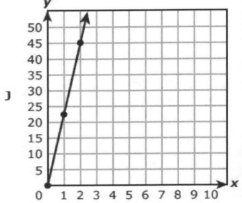

54.   An inequality is shown.

$$\frac{1}{8} < x < 18\%$$

Which value of x makes the inequality true?

A. $\frac{1}{5}$

B. 1.6

C. 0.09

D. $\sqrt{0.02}$

55.   Pinto and Emma are selling ribbons to raise money for the football team. The graph shows the linear relationship between the number of ribbons each of them has left to sell and the number of days that they have been selling ribbons.

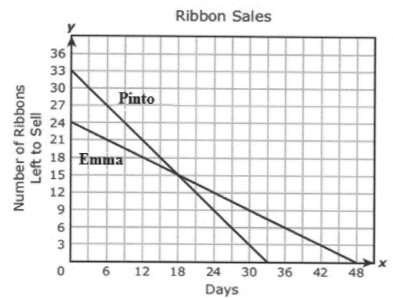

On which day, does it appear that Frank and Erica will have the same number of ribbons left to sell?

A. Day 15

B. Day 48

C. Day 33

D. Day 18

56.   The value of y varies directly with x. When y = 75, $x = 9$ What is the value of y when x is 6?

A. 72

B. 50

C. 0.72

D. Not here

57. Which table contains only corresponding x-values and y-values where x is twice that of y?

A.

x	y
7	5
10	6.5
14	8.5
17	10

C.

x	y
7	3.5
10	5
14	7
17	8.5

B.

x	y
7	6.5
10	8
14	10
17	11.5

D.

x	y
7	14
10	20
14	28
17	34

58. Which situation represents a proportional relationship?
A. The cost of purchasing a basket of oranges for $1.30 per pound plus $5.00 for the basket.
B. The cost of purchasing peaches for $7.00 per box of peaches with a delivery charge of $3.00.
C. The cost of purchasing grapefruit for $1.80 per pound.
D. The cost of purchasing apples for $1.75 per pound plus a shipping fee of $0.16 per pound.

59.   Which set of ordered pairs represents y as a function of x?
       A. {(2, −1) (4, −2), (6, −3), (8, −4)}
       B. {(0, 0), (1, 1), (1, 0), (2, 1)}
       C. {(3, 3), (3, 4), (4, 3), (4, 4)}
       D. {(1, −5), (1, 5), (2, −10), (2, −15)}

60.   The model represents an equation.

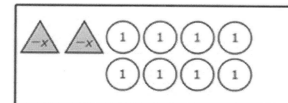 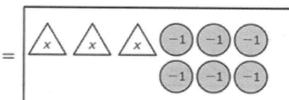

       What value of x makes the equation true?

61. A tree in Dante's neighborhood grew 18 inches in the first 2 years after it was planted. If the tree continues to grow at this same rate, which graph best represents the growth rate of the tree in inches per year?

F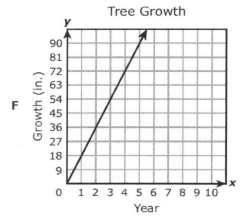

H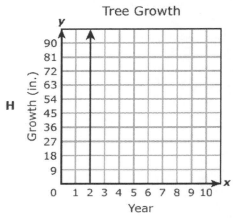

G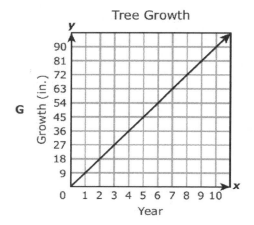

J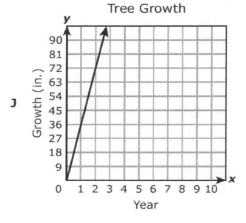

62. Mr. Vinci is renting a car for one day. The table below shows the total amount he will be charged for the car based on the number of miles he drives.

Car Rental

Name of Miles, m	Total Amount Charged, c
5	$30.50
10	$31.00
15	$31.50
20	$32.00

Which equation best represents c, the number of dollars Mr. Vinci should be charged for driving m miles?

A. c = 0.10m + 30

B. c = 30m + 0.10

C. c = 0.50m + 30

D. c = 30m + 0.50

63. Sheeran will buy the same number of stamps every month to add to a stamp collection her grandfather gave her. The table represents the number of stamps Sheeran will have at the end of x months.

Sheeran 's Stamp Collection

Number of Months, X	1	3	6	10
Number of Stamps, Y	250	350	500	700

How many stamps was Sheeran given, and how many stamps will she buy every month?
A. Sheeran was given 200 stamps, and she will buy 50 stamps every month.
B. Sheeran was given 250 stamps, and she will buy 50 stamps every month.
C. Sheeran was given 225 stamps, and she will buy 25 stamps every month.
D. Sheeran was given 200 stamps, and she will buy 25 stamps every month.

64. Artisan Fest A charges an entrance fee of $5.00 and $0.65 per ticket for the rides. Fest B charges an entrance fee of $10.00 and $0.45 per ticket for the rides. How many tickets must be purchased in order for the total cost at Fest A and Fest B to be the same?
A. 25
B. 10
C. 50
D. 75

65. Shail is ordering trophies for her school. Company A charges $4.50 for each trophy and a one-time engraving fee of $30. Company B charges $8.50 for each trophy and a one-time engraving fee of $21. Which inequality can be used to find x, the minimum number of trophies that can be ordered so that the total charge at Company A is less than the total charge at Company B?

A. $4.50 + 30x < 8.50 + 21x$

B. $4.50 + 30x > 8.50 + 21x$

C. $4.50x + 30 < 8.50x + 21$

D. $4.50x + 30 > 8.50x + 21$

66. An inequality is shown.

$$\frac{1}{80} < x < 1.8\%$$

Which value of x makes the inequality true?

A. $\frac{1}{5}$

B. 1.6

C. 0.09

D. 1.5%

67. Which graph shows a non-proportional linear relationship between x and y?

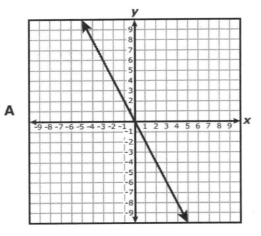

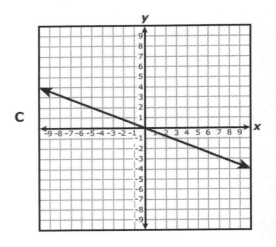

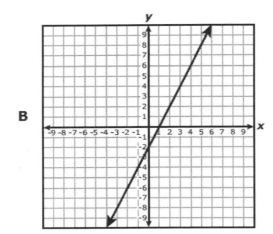

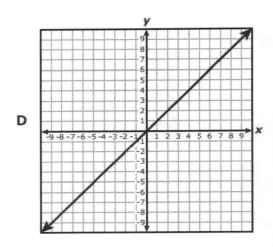

68. Which set of ordered pairs represents y as a function of x?

A. {(2, 1), (3, 1), (2, 1), (4, 1)}

B. {(3, 2), (4, 3), (5, 2), (2, 6)}

C. {(1, 3), (3, 5), (2, 5), (1, 6)}

D. {(4, 7), (4, 6), (4, 4), (4, 1)}

69.   Malishka is saving $25 which she earned for washing her mom's car. She earns $10 every week for doing other chores, which she also saves.

Which function can be used to find t, the amount of money Malishka will have saved at the end of n weeks of doing chores?

A. $t = 10n + 25$

B. $t = 25n + 10$

C. $t = 35n$

D. $t = 15n$

70.   Emily sells greeting cards. The graph models the linear relationship between the number of boxes of cards she sells and her profit.

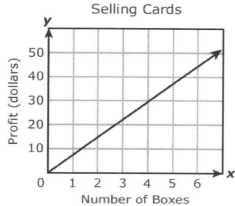

Which of these best describes the profit Emily makes from selling these cards?

A. $7.50 per box

B. $10.00 per box

C. $4.00 per 30 boxes

D. $3.00 per 4 boxes

71. Which points on the coordinate grid blow satisfy the conditions $x > -3\frac{1}{2}$ and $y < 1\frac{4}{5}$?

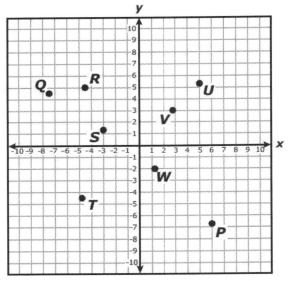

A. Points P and U

B. Points Q, R, and T

C. Points Q, S, T, and W

D. Points P, S, and W

72. Find the constant of proportionality from the table below.

X	7.5	10	17.5	20
Y	4.5	6	10.5	12

73. Find the constant of proportionality from the table below.

X	1.5	2.5	3.5	10
Y	10.5	17.5	24.5	70

74.   Andrea rents a bike for a day. The rental charges can be determined by the equation: R = 0.5d, where R is rental charges and d is number of days she rents the bike. Calculate the unit rate.

75.   Find the constant of proportionality from the equations below.
0.5y = 7.25x

76.   The perimeter of a rectangle is 40 inches. If the length of the rectangle is 11 inches, which equation could be used to find the width, x?
A. $11(x + 2) = 40$
B. $x + 2(11) = 40$
C. $x + 11 = 40$
D. $2(x + 11) = 40$

77.   Which of the following can be represented by the inequality below?
$$64M + 163 \geq 1,123$$
    A. Jamal wants to save at most $1,123. He has already saved $163 and deposited $64 every month into his savings account.
    B. Jamal wants to save more than $1,123. He has already saved $64 and deposited $163 every month into his savings account.
    C. Jamal wants to save at least $1,123. He has already saved $163 and deposited $64 every month into his savings account.
    D. Not here

78.   Find the constant of proportionality from the equations below:
$0.5y - 3x = 0$

79.   Solve linear inequality.
$$2 - 5(x + 1) \geq 3(x - 1) - 8$$
    A. $1 \geq x$
    B. $x \leq -1$
    C. $x \leq 1$
    D. None of the above

80. The data in the table below represents the relationship between the radius of a circle in inches, *x*, and the approximate circumference of the circle in inches, *y*.

Radius and Circumference

Radius, x (in)	Circumference, y (in)
1	6.28
2	12.56
3	18.84
4	25.12

Which graph best represents the data in the table above?

A.

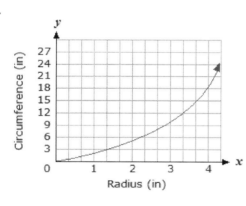

B.

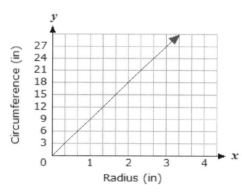

C.

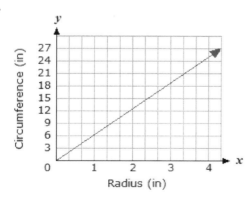

D.

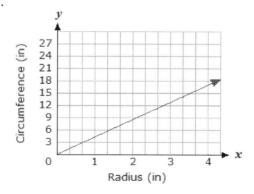

81. An architect presented a drawing to a client that had the following scale.

$$\frac{2}{3} \text{in} = 8 \text{ ft}$$

Which graph below best represents this relationship?

A.

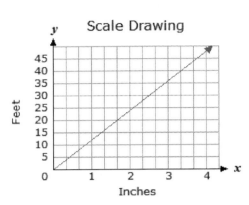

B.

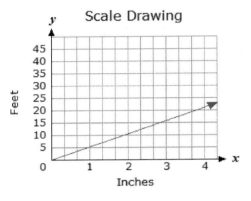

C.

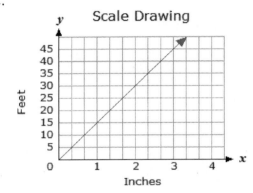

D.

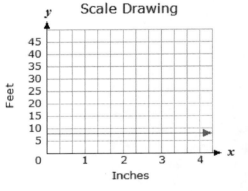

82. Which of the following CANNOT be used to find the perimeter of an equilateral triangle with side length 's'?

A. $2s + s$

B. $3s$

C. $\frac{1}{2}s \times s$

D. $s + s + s$

83. A walking trail was built around a circular grassy area in a park, as shown in the drawing below.

The circumference of the grassy area is two-thirds of the circumference of the outside border of the walking trail.

If the radius of the grassy area is 30 meters, which equation could be used to find R, the radius of the outside border of the walking trail?

A. $\frac{2}{3} \cdot 30 = \pi \cdot R$

B. $\frac{2}{3}(30) = R$

C. $\frac{3}{2} \cdot \pi = 30 \cdot R$

D. $\frac{3}{2}(30) = R$

84. Which equation uses the diameter of a circle, d, in order to find the area of the circle, A?

A. $A = \pi \left(\frac{d}{2}\right)^2$

B. $a = \left(\frac{d}{2}\right)^2 + \pi$

C. $A = d\pi$

D. $A = 2d\pi$

85. The design of a necklace pendant is made up of one larger circle and two smaller circles, as shown in the drawing below.

If each smaller circle has a circumference of 163 mm, which equation could be used to find R, the radius of the larger circle?

A. $\frac{163}{\pi} \cdot 2 = R$

B. $\frac{163}{\pi} = R$

C. $\frac{163}{\pi} = 2R$

D. $163 = \pi \cdot R \cdot 2$

86.   Which equation best fits the data?

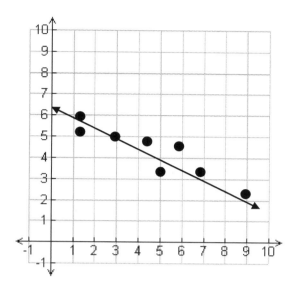

A. $y = \frac{1}{2}x + 6.5$

B. $y = -\frac{1}{2}x + 6.5$

C. $y = -5x - 6$

D. $y = 3x - 6.5$

87.   You want to rent a bus for a trip to the city. The bus costs $600 for the night and $0.25 per mile. You have $800 to spend. Write an inequality that represents this scenario.

A. $600 + 0.25x < 800$

B. $600 + 0.25x > 800$

C. $600 + 0.25x \leq 800$

D. $600x + 0.25 \leq 800$

88.   Which scatter plot has positive correlation?

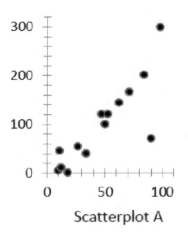

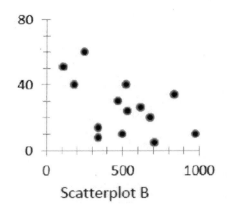

A. Scatter plot A

B. Scatter plot B

C. Both

D. None

89.   Jen jogged at a constant pace. After $2\frac{1}{2}$ hours, she had jogged 10 miles. If you were to graph the line of this proportional relationship between distance jogged and time, which of the following pairs of coordinates represent points on the line?

E. (1, 4) and (2, 10)

F. $\left(2\frac{1}{2}, 10\right)$ and (1, 5)

G. (1, 4) and (2, 8)

H. $\left(2\frac{1}{2}, 10\right)$ and (5, 15)

90. The table shows the amount of money Kenneth saved each month. If you were to graph the line of this proportional relationship, what is the slope and what does it represent?

Number of Months	Total Amount of Savings ($)
2	70
3	105
4	140

    A. 35; Kenneth saved $35 per month.
    B. 70; Kenneth saved $70 per month.
    C. 105; Kenneth saved $105 per month.
    D. 140; Kenneth saved $140 per month.

91. The slope of a line is $-\frac{1}{2}$. One point on the line is $(-2, 9)$. What is another point on the line?
    A. $(-4, 10)$
    B. $(1, 6)$
    C. $(2, -9)$
    D. $(4, 8)$

92. Which equation does NOT show a proportional relationship?
    A. $y - 2 = 0.5x - 2$
    B. $y - 4 = 2x - 4$
    C. $y = -0.4x - 3$
    D. $y + 5 = 5x + 5$

93.   What is the equation for the values in the table?

x	-10	-5	5	10
y	-3	-1	3	5

A. $y = -\dfrac{2}{5}x - 1$

B. $y = \dfrac{5}{2}x + 1$

C. $y = \dfrac{2}{5}x + 1$

D. $y = \dfrac{1}{2}x - \dfrac{1}{2}$

94.   Which relation shown in the graph is NOT a function?

A.
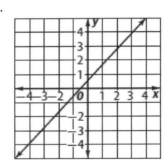

B.
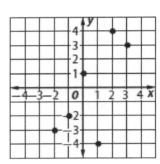

C.
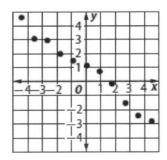

D.
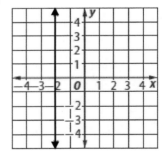

95.   Solve for h.

$$-5.6 = \frac{h}{5} + 12.2$$

96.   The line graphed below represents the elevation of a car as it drives down a hill.

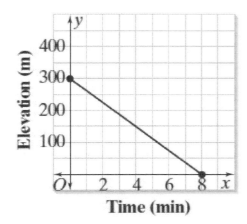

Which statement below appears to be true if the slope of the line was doubled?

A. The hill would be twice as tall.

B. The hill would be half as tall.

C. The car would be moving twice as fast.

D. The car would be moving half as fast.

97.   A phone company charges $30.00 per month plus $1 for every minute of long distance phone calls. The total charge is graphed below.

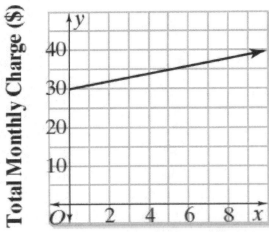

Long Distance Call Time (min)

Which of the following will increase the charges if monthly charges are increased to $40?

A. Slope

B. y-intercept

C. Both

D. None

98.   Each month, Rebecca adds money to her bank account. The amount of money in Rebecca's bank account is graphed below.

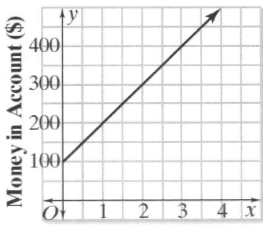

If the y-intercept of this graph were changed to 75, what would change in the situation?

A. Rebecca would have added $75 more to her bank account each month.

B. Rebecca would have started with $75 more in her bank account.

C. Rebecca would have started with $25 less in her bank account.

D. Rebecca would have added $25 less to her bank account each month.

99.   Megan uses $\frac{2}{3}$ cup of almonds to make 4 cups of trail mix. Using this same proportion, how many cups of almonds would Megan need to make 9 cups of trail mix?

A. $1\frac{1}{2}$ cups

B. $1\frac{7}{12}$ cups

C. $2\frac{11}{12}$ cups

D. $3\frac{3}{8}$ cups

100.   Which equation represents the following sentence?

The sum of the product of one-fourth and a number and the product of two-fifths and another number is twelve.

A. $\frac{1}{4}x - \frac{2}{5}y = 12$

B. $\frac{1}{4}x + \frac{2}{5}y = 12$

C. $\frac{13}{20}(x + y) = 12$

D. $\left(\frac{1}{4} + x\right)\left(\frac{2}{5} + y\right) = 12$

Answer Key

		Marks (C/W)
1	158	
2	B	
3	D	
4	C	
5	B	
6	A	
7	B	
8	B	
9	B	
10	A	
11	D	
12	B	
13	C	
14	C	
15	C	
16	B	
17	D	
18	C	
19	D	
20	B	
21	B	
22	A	
23	B	
24	C	
25	D	
26	A	
27	A	
28	A	
29	D	
30	C	
31	A	
32	C	
33	C	
34	B	
	Total	

		Marks (C/W)
35	G	
36	2.25	
37	C	
38	C	
39	G	
40	H	
41	C	
42	D	
43	C	
44	F	
45	C	
46	F	
47	B	
48	D	
49	A	
50	27	
51	C	
52	A	
53	J	
54	D	
55	D	
56	B	
57	C	
58	C	
59	A	
60	2.8	
61	G	
62	A	
63	A	
64	A	
65	C	
66	D	
67	B	
68	B	
	Total	

		Marks (C/W)
69	A	
70	A	
71	D	
72	0.6	
73	7	
74	0.5	
75	14.5	
76	D	
77	C	
78	6	
79	C	
80	C	
81	A	
82	C	
83	D	
84	A	
85	B	
86	B	
87	C	
88	A	
89	G	
90	A	
91	A	
92	C	
93	C	
94	D	
95	-89	
96	C	
97	B	
98	C	
99	A	
100	B	
101		
102		
	Total	

SECTION 3

GEOMETRY, MEASUREMENT AND SPATIAL REASONING

1. Gerrard drew $\overline{CD}$ in isosceles trapezoid *AEFB* to create similar trapezoids *AEFB* and *CEFD*.

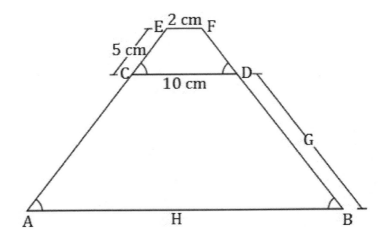

Based on the given information, what are the values of *G* and H in centimeters?

A. *G* = 13 cm and *H* = 18 cm

B. *G* = 25 cm and *H* = 50 cm

C. *G* = 10 cm and *H* = 50 cm

D. *G* = 15 cm and *H* = 27 cm

2. Solve for the value of x given that l$_1$ is parallel to l$_2$.

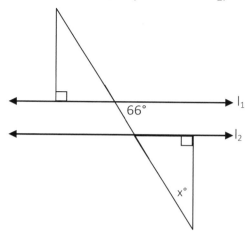

3. Pentagon IFGHJ is similar to pentagon PTSRQ. The perimeter of the pentagon IFGHJ is 47.4 centimeters.

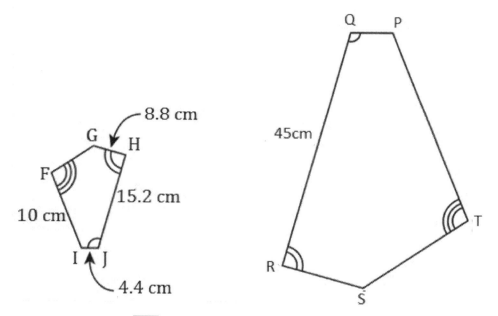

What is the length of $\overline{ST}$ rounded to the nearest tenth?

A. 18.8 cm

B. 26.6 cm

C. 20.2 cm

D. Not here

4. Sania has a birdhouse with rectangular walls, a rectangular bottom, and a rectangular entry, like the one modeled below.

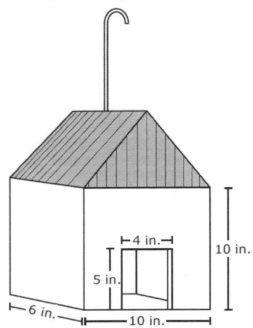

She will paint the four outside walls but not the bottom or the roof of the birdhouse. What is the area that Sania will paint?

A. 320 in.²

B. 160 in.²

C. 300 in.²

D. 140 in.²

5. Polygon *ADCB* below was dilated by a scale factor of $\frac{9}{5}$ to create polygon A'D'C'B'.

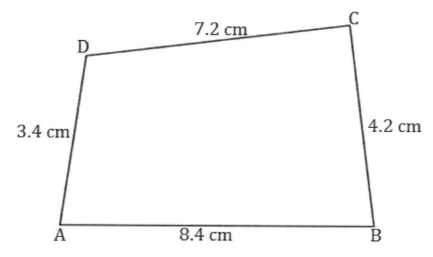

What is the length of $\overline{D'C'}$ in centimeters?

6. The bases of the two similar triangular prisms shown below are equilateral triangles.

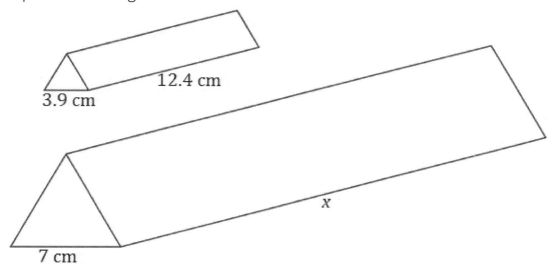

What is the value of x, an edge length of the larger prism in centimeters if rounded to the nearest hundredths?

7.   Triangle *PQR* is similar to triangle *ABC*.

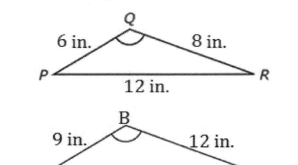

What is the length of *AC*?

A. 15 in.

B. 13.5 in.

C. 18 in.

D. 20.25 in.

8.   According to the Austin Parks and Wildlife Department, there are about 35 black-tailed deer per square mile in each of 40 Texas counties. A rectangular area on a ranch in one of these counties measures 3.25 miles by 7.2 miles. Which of the following is closest to the number of black-tailed deer expected to be living in this rectangular area?

A. 480

B. 820

C. 720

D. 600

9. In the drawing below, the dashed line segment represents the distance across a pond.

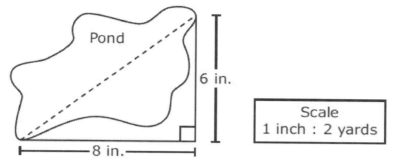

What is the actual distance, in yards, across the pond?

10. Pentagon *DEABC* below models one side of a building.

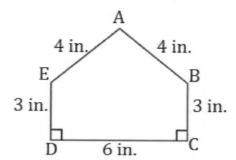

The sum of the interior angles of the pentagon is 540°, the measure of angle *A* is 100°, and ∠*E* ≅ ∠*B*. What is the measure of ∠*E*?

A. 92°

B. 130°

C. 108°

D. Not here

11. A regular pentagon is dilated by a scale factor of $\frac{3}{2}$ to create a new pentagon. Which of the following statements is true?

   A. The perimeter of the new pentagon is $\frac{9}{4}$ times the perimeter of the original pentagon.

   B. The perimeter of the new pentagon is $\frac{9}{2}$ times the perimeter of the original pentagon.

   C. The perimeter of the new pentagon is $\frac{15}{2}$ times the perimeter of the original pentagon.

   D. The perimeter of the new pentagon is $\frac{3}{2}$ times the perimeter of the original pentagon.

12. A rectangle has a length of 7.5 inches and a width of 3 inches. This rectangle is dilated by a scale factor of 2.2 to create a new rectangle. Which figure represents the new rectangle?

A.

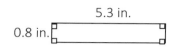

5.3 in.

0.8 in.

B.

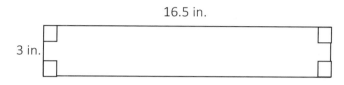

16.5 in.

3 in.

C.

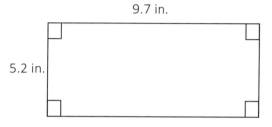

9.7 in.

5.2 in.

D.

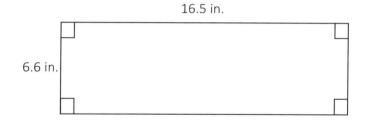

16.5 in.

6.6 in.

13. The figure shows a triangle inside a circle. Which procedure should be used to find the area of the shaded region?

   A. Find the perimeter of the triangle, and then subtract the circumference of the circle.
   B. Find the area of the triangle, and then subtract the area of the circle.
   C. Find the circumference of the circle, and then subtract the perimeter of the triangle.
   D. Find the area of the circle, and then subtract the area of the triangle.

14. The number of diagonals that can be drawn in polygon with n sides can be determined by $\frac{n(n-3)}{2}$. How man diagonals can be drawn in a polygon with 9 sides?
   A. 18
   B. 27
   C. 39
   D. 54

15. The diameter of the New York state seal is approximately 4 inches. What is the approximate circumference of the seal?
   A. 3.14 in.
   B. 6.28 in.
   C. 12.56 in.
   D. 14 in.

16. The diagram below shows the pool and deck area in Roma's backyard. The dimensions of the deck are shown in the diagram.

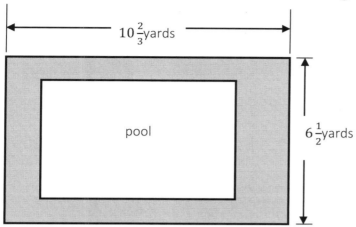

What is the perimeter of the deck in Roma's backyard?

A. $32\frac{1}{6}$ yards

B. $34\frac{1}{6}$ yards

C. $34\frac{1}{3}$ yards

D. $69\frac{1}{3}$ yards

17. Mrs. Saturn's dog is kept on a 10-feet chain attached to a stake in the center of the backyard. The backyard property is a 30-feet by 50-feet rectangle. Approximately how much of the backyard is NOT accessible by the dog when it is attached to the chain?

A. 314 ft²

B. 1186 ft²

C. 1500 ft²

D. 1814 ft²

18. What is the perimeter of a square dog pen with an area of 36 square yards?

    A. 28 yards

    B. 12 yards

    C. 9 yards

    D. 24 yards

19. The sum of the interior angles of a triangle is 180°. The sum of the interior angles of a rectangle is 360°. The sum of the interior angles of a pentagon is 540°. What is the sum of the interior angles of a decagon if same pattern continues?

    A. 630°

    B. 1440°

    C. 900°

    D. 1,080°

20.   The areas of three circles are shown.

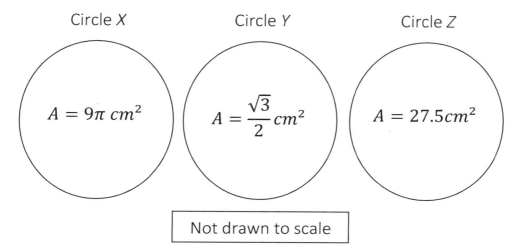

Circle X

$A = 9\pi \ cm^2$

Circle Y

$A = \dfrac{\sqrt{3}}{2} cm^2$

Circle Z

$A = 27.5 cm^2$

Not drawn to scale

Which list shows the circles in order from biggest radius to smallest radius?

A. Circle Z, circle Y, circle X

B. Circle Y, circle Z, circle X

C. Circle X, circle Z, circle Y

D. Circle X, circle Y, circle Z

21. Triangle *DEF* and triangle *GHI* are similar right triangles.

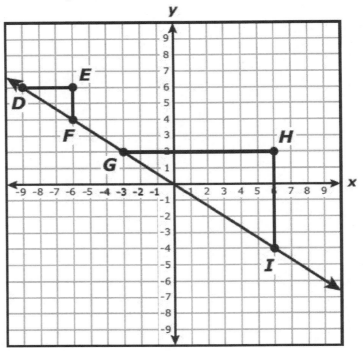

Based on this information, which statement is true?

A. The relationship between the slope of the hypotenuse of triangle *DEF* and the slope of the hypotenuse of triangle *GHI* cannot be determined.

B. The slope of the hypotenuse of triangle *DEF* is greater than the slope of the hypotenuse of triangle *GHI*.

C. The slope of the hypotenuse of triangle *DEF* is less than the slope of the hypotenuse of triangle *GHI*.

D. The slope of the hypotenuse of triangle *DEF* is equal to the slope of the hypotenuse of triangle *GHI*.

22. Which measurements can**not** represent the side lengths of a right triangle?

   A. 6 cm, 8 cm, 10 cm

   B. 12 cm, 35 cm, 37 cm

   C. 4 cm, 6 cm, 10 cm

   D. 10 cm, 24 cm, 26 cm

23. In each diagram, line *p* is parallel to line *f*, and line *t* intersects lines *p* and *f*.

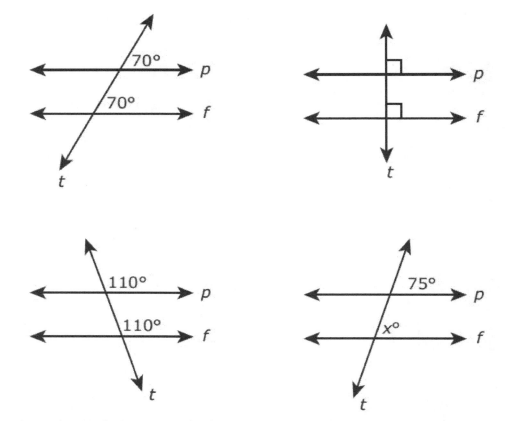

Based on these diagrams, which statement is true?

A. The value of *x* should be 75, because the angles shown in the diagrams are congruent.

B. The value of *x* should be 105, because the measures of the angles shown in the diagrams add up to 180°.

C. The value of *x* should be 140, because the measures of the angles shown in the diagrams should add up to 360° and 360–(110+110) = 140.

D. The value of *x* should be 70, because the measures of the angles shown in the diagrams are both 70°.

24. Quadrilateral *ABCD* is transformed according to the rule
$(x, y) \rightarrow (x+9, y + 4)$ to create quadrilateral *A'B'C'D'*.

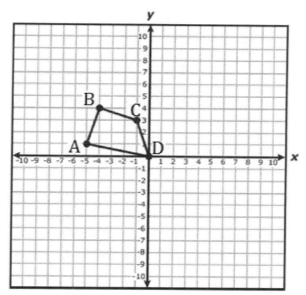

Which statement is true?

A. The side lengths of quadrilateral *A'B'C'D'* are twice the corresponding side lengths of quadrilateral *ABCD*.

B. The angle measures of quadrilateral *A'B'C'D'* are equal to the corresponding angle measures of quadrilateral *ABCD*.

C. The side lengths of quadrilateral *A'B'C'D'* are 9 units longer than the corresponding side lengths of quadrilateral *ABCD*.

D. The angle measures of quadrilateral *A'B'C'D'* are greater than the corresponding angle measures of quadrilateral *ABCD*.

25. A transformation is applied to a figure to create a new figure. Which transformation does **not** preserve congruence?

A. A reflection across the *x*-axis

B. A translation 7 units down

C. A dilation by a scale factor of 5

D. A rotation of 90° clockwise

26.   What is the measure of ∠S in the figure at the right?

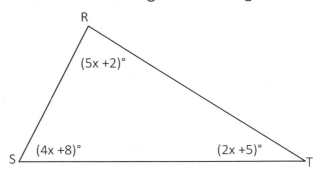

A. 55°

B. 59°

C. 68°

D. 74°

27.   The figure below shows a smaller square inside a larger square. What is the area of the smaller square?

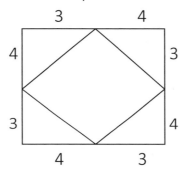

Figure is not drawn to scale

A. 9 units²

B. 25 units²

C. 36 units²

D. 49 units²

28.   On a sunny day, a two-feet tall tree casts a shadow six feet long. At the same time, a nearby tree casts a shadow 42 feet long.

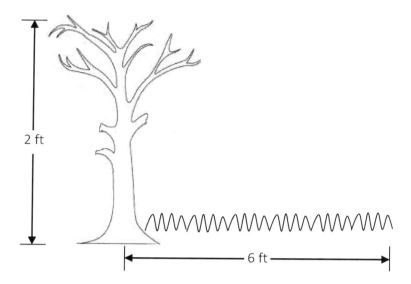

What is the height of the taller tree?

A. 12 ft

B. 14 ft

C. 16 ft

D. 18 ft

29. The diagram below shows the path of a ball that is dropped from a height of 27 feet. What is the rebound height after the 4th bounce?

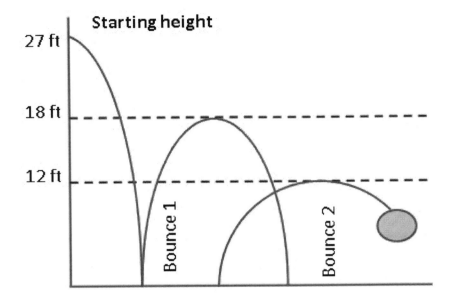

A. 18 ft

B. 12 ft

C. 8 ft

D. $5\frac{1}{3} ft$

30. Which triangle is similar to the triangle given?

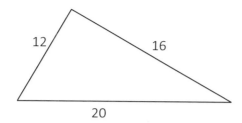

A.

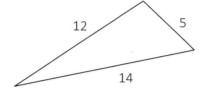

B.

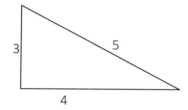

C.

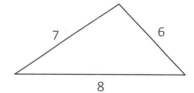

D.

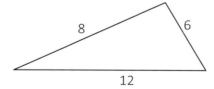

31. The figure below shows the tent that Vicky's scout troop will sleep in when they go for camping. How wide is the bottom front of the tent if 3 ft is height of bottom front?

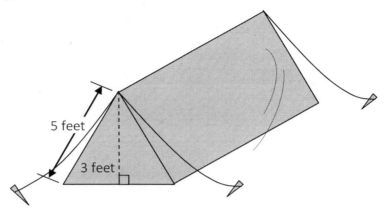

5 feet

3 feet

A. 4 ft
B. 5 ft
C. 6 ft
D. 8 ft

32. A contractor built a scale replica of a proposed new shopping mall. The replica's parking lot is 13 inches wide by 20 inches long. If the actual mall parking lot will be 100 yards long, what will be its area?
A. 65 yd²
B. 100 yd²
C. 1300 yd²
D. 6500 yd²

33. Parallelogram *ABCD* is a dilation of parallelogram *WXYZ*.

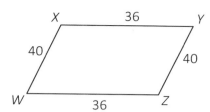 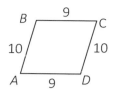

What scale factor was used to reduce *WXYZ* to *ABCD*?

A. 4

B. 0.8

C. 0.25

D. 0.2

34. For an art display, Nadal ordered a circular wall hanging with a radius of 5 feet. The wall hanging costs $1.50 per square foot. Which of the following is a reasonable estimate for the cost of the wall hanging?

A. $128.00

B. $144.00

C. $149.00

D. $117.75

35. A circular helipad has a circumference of 63 feet. What is the circumference of the circular warning area, whose diameter is twice that of the helipad?

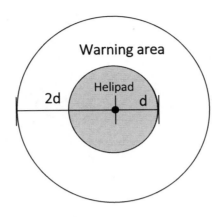

A. 110 ft

B. 126 ft

C. 252 ft

D. 504 ft

36. In the triangle below, what is the approximate length of side *AB*?

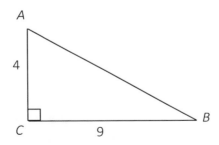

A. Between 5 and 6

B. Between 8 and 9

C. Between 9 and 10

D. Between 10 and 11

37.   The parallelograms below are similar.

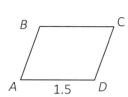
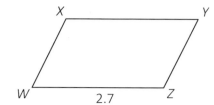

What scale factor is used to dilate parallelogram *ABCD* to parallelogram *WXYZ*?

A. 1.5

B. 1.6

C. 1.8

D. 2.7

38. For which triangle does the relationship
a² + b² = c² fit?

A.

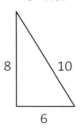

B.

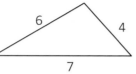

C.

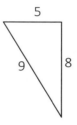

D.

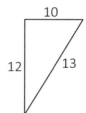

39. These trapezoids are similar. What is the length of side *x*?

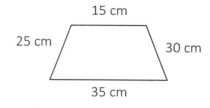
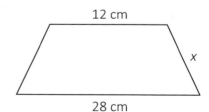

A. 15 cm

B. 18 cm

C. 20 cm

D. 24 cm

40.   What is the measure of the larger of two complementary angles if the measure of one angle is five times the measure of the other angle?
        A. 15°
        B. 16°
        C. 74°
        D. 75°

41.   The table shows the total number of diagonals in a convex polygon with n sides.

Number of Sides	4	5	6	n
Number of Diagonals	2	5	9	$\frac{1}{2}n(n-3)$

        How many diagonal does an octagon have?
        A. 16
        B. 18
        C. 20
        D. 24

42.   Katie wants to frame a painting of the Alamo. The painting is 14 inches long and 12 inches wide. If she places a 3-inches frame around the painting, what will be the dimensions of the outside edge of the frame?
        A. 28 in. × 24 in.
        B. 20 in. × 18 in.
        C. 17 in. × 15 in.
        D. 11 in. × 9 in.

43. A right triangle has a perimeter of 30 centimeters. The length of each side is increased to 5 times its original length. What is the perimeter of the larger triangle?

    A. 60 cm

    B. 90 cm

    C. 150 cm

    D. 300 cm

44. Shanaya owns a drum that has a diameter of 16 inches and a height of 7.5 inches, as shown below. She wants to design a new drum by dilating the dimensions of the original drum by a scale factor of 1.8.

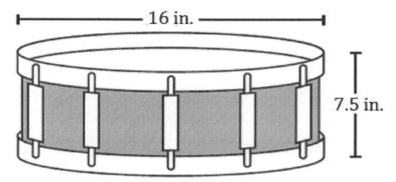

    What will be the diameter, *d*, and the height, *h*, of the new drum?

    A. *d* = 28.8 in. and *h* = 13.5 in.

    B. *d* = 25.4 in. and *h* = 16.9 in.

    C. *d* = 12.5 in. and *h* = 4 in.

    D. *d* = 22.5 in. and *h* = 14 in.

45. A paper drinking cup in the shape of a cone has a height of 22 centimeters and a volume of 1,129 cubic centimeter. Which of the following is closest to the diameter of the cup in centimeters?
    A. 11 cm
    B. 14 cm
    C. 16 cm
    D. 15 cm

46. The roof of a house is in the shape of a square pyramid. The slant height of the pyramid is 17 feet, and the length of each side of the square is 30 feet. What is the lateral surface area of the pyramid in square feet?
    A. 1, 920 ft²
    B. 2, 040 ft²
    C. 1, 020 ft²
    D. 1, 410 ft²

47. A ball shaped like a sphere has a radius of approximately $2\frac{1}{8}$ inches. Which of the following is the best estimate of the volume of the ball?
    A. 38in³
    B. 11in³
    C. 25in.³
    D. 17in³

48. A cube is dilated by a scale factor of $\frac{3}{4}$ to create a new cube. The surface area of the new cube is —

    A. $\frac{3}{2}$ the surface area of the original cube

    B. $\frac{27}{64}$ the surface are of the original cube

    C. $\frac{9}{16}$ the surface area of the original cube

    D. $\frac{9}{4}$ the surface are of the original cube

49. Mike used the expression below to find the volume, in cubic centimeters, of a square pyramid.

$$\frac{1}{3}(12^2)(14)$$

Which square pyramid has a volume equal to the value of the expression Mike wrote?

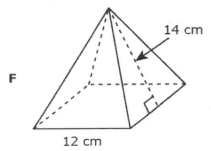
F
14 cm
12 cm

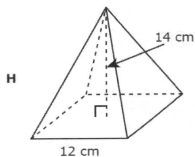
H
14 cm
12 cm

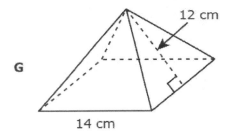
G
12 cm
14 cm

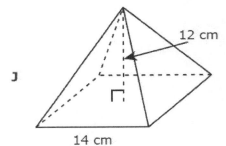
J
12 cm
14 cm

50. Yonita covered the outside of a gift box shaped like a rectangular prism with paper. The box is 3.6 feet long, 2.4 feet wide and 2.8 feet high. Which of the following is closest to the total surface area of this box?

A. 34 ft²

B. 42 ft²

C. 30 ft²

D. 51 ft²

51. A sphere is dilated by a scale factor of 1.16 to create a new sphere. How does the volume of the new sphere compare with the volume of the original sphere?

A. The volume of the new sphere is 1.16 times the volume of the original sphere.

B. The volume of the new sphere is $(1.16)^3$ times the volume of the original sphere.

C. The volume of the new sphere is $(1.16)^2$ times the volume of the original sphere.

D. The volume of the new sphere is $(2.32)^2$ times the volume of the original sphere.

52. A water heater has a diameter of 18 inches. It sits in a drain pan that has a diameter of 22 inches and a height of 2 inches, as modeled in the diagram below.

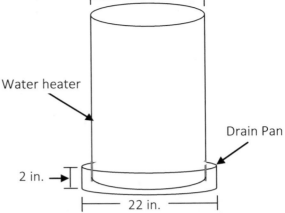

Water that leaks out of the water heater accumulates in the drain pan. Which of the following is closest to the maximum amount of water that the drain pan can contain with the water heater in the position shown?

A. 13 in³

B. 1,005 in³

C. 251 in³

D. 50 in³

53. A rectangular pool is 5 meters long, 6 meters wide and 2 meters deep. If water fills the pool at a rate of 5 cubic meters per hour, how long will it take for the pool to be half full?

A. 2 hours

B. 6 hours

C. 12 hours

D. 15 hours

54. The two rectangles forming the roof of the house below are congruent. A roofing company charges $1.50 per square foot to shingle a roof.

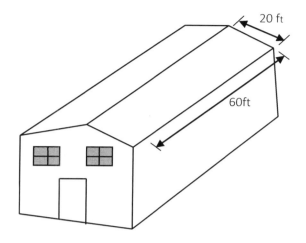

What will be the cost for shingling the roof of the house?
A. $1200
B. $1800
C. $2400
D. $3600

55. The figure below is the net of a cylinder.

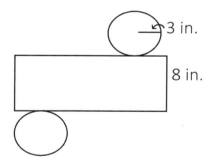

What is the lateral surface area of the cylinder to the nearest tenth?
A. 47.2 in²
B. 122.5 in²
C. 141.4 in²
D. 150.7 in²

56.   What happens to the volume of a cube when the dimension of each side is doubled?

A. The volume is eight times the original volume.

B. The volume is twice the original volume.

C. The volume is four times the original volume.

D. The volume remains same.

57.   Jonita's architecture class built a square pyramid out of plywood. They plan to paint the outside of the pyramid, including the bottom. The pyramid has the dimensions shown below.

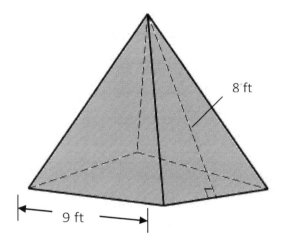

What is the total surface area of the pyramid?

A. 216 square feet

B. 184 square feet

C. 225 square feet

D. 204 square feet

58. Garbage and recycling Collection Company distributed recycling bins to its customers. Each bin is a rectangular prism that has a square base 4 feet long on each side and a volume of 24 cubic feet. How tall is each bin?
    A. 1.5 ft
    B. 2 ft
    C. 3 ft
    D. 4 ft

59. A square flag is folded in half to form a right triangle. Which statement about the triangle is true?
    A. The measure of longest side of the triangle is same as edge of the flag.
    B. The square of the height of the triangle is equal to the sum of the squares of the edge length of the flag.
    C. The sum of the edge lengths is equal to the length of the fold.
    D. The sum of the squares of the edge lengths is equal to the square of the length of the fold.

60.　Mr. Anthem wishes to paint his warehouse. He needs to calculate the lateral surface area of the warehouse so that he will know how much paint he has to buy. The warehouse is in the shape of a rectangular prism with the dimensions shown below.

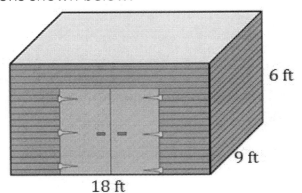

Including the doors, what is the lateral surface area of the storage warehouse in square feet?

A. 972 ft²

B. 648 ft²

C. 532 ft²

D. 324 ft²

61.　The diameter of a table tennis ball is 4 centimeters. How many square centimeters of plastic are needed to make a table tennis ball?

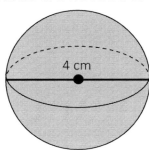

A. 42.4 cm²

B. 50.3 cm²

C. 77.6 cm²

D. 201.1 cm²

62.   The dimensions of two similar desk drawers are shown below.

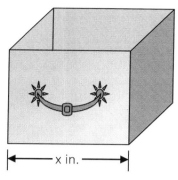 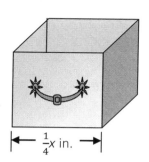

The volume of the larger drawer is 4,096 square inches. What is the volume of the smaller drawer?

A. 2,048 in³

B. 1,024 in³

C. 256 in³

D. 64 in³

63. A fire extinguisher is $16\frac{4}{5}$ inches tall and has a radius of $3\frac{4}{7}$ inches.

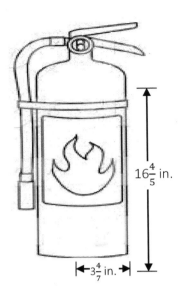

What is the volume of the fire extinguisher?

A. 281π in³

B. $154\frac{4}{7}\pi$ in³

C. $252\frac{3}{5}\pi$ in³

D. $214\frac{2}{7}\pi$ in³

64. Which of the following formulas can be used to find the volume of the figure below, where the base has an area of 8 square inches?

A. $V = \frac{1}{3}8h$

B. $V = 8h$

C. $V = 8lwh$

D. $V = \frac{4}{3}8h$

65. Marissa is having her office walls repainted. She needs to calculate the square footage of the wall surfaces. The dimensions of the office are shown on the diagram below.

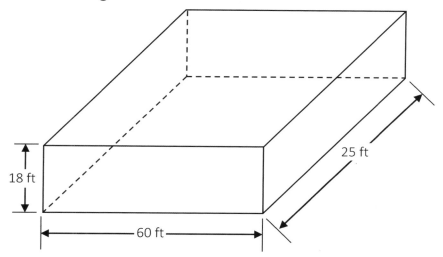

What is the surface area of the walls?
A. 3060 ft²
B. 2500 ft²
C. 1600 ft²
D. 1000ft²

66.   Rachel drew a floor plan for her new kitchen.

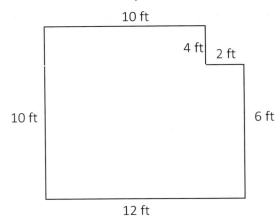

What is the area of the kitchen floor?
A. 96 ft²
B. 112 ft²
C. 124 ft²
D. 140 ft²

67.   Circle S has a radius that is twice the radius of circle T.

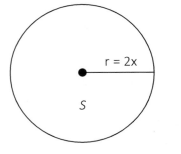 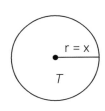

Which statement is true about the relationship of the areas of circles S and T?
A. The area of circle S is 4 times the area of circle T.
B. The area of circle S is 2 times the area of circle T.
C. The area of circle S is $\frac{1}{2}$ the area of circle T.
D. The area of circle S is $\frac{1}{4}$ the area of circle T.

68. The combined triangular bases of the solid figure below have an area of 230 square inches. Which of the following formulas can be used to find out the volume of the figure if 'h' is height of the figure?

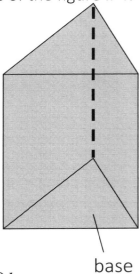

base

A. $V = \frac{1}{3}(230)h$

B. $V = \frac{1}{6}(230)h$

C. $V = 115h$

D. $V = 115Bh$

69. Samuel found the cylindrical can shown in the figure below in his recycling bin. He plans to use it for a craft project and needs to cover the side and bottom with construction paper.

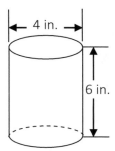

Approximately how many square inches of paper will Samuel need if there is no overlap?

A. 75 in²

B. 88 in²

C. 150 in²

D. 201 in²

70. The area of a square is 275 square meters. Which best represents the length of a side of the square?

A. 16.5 m

B. 51.8 m

C. 14.1 m

D. 68.75 m

71. The cone and the cylinder have the same base diameter and the same height. How many times more is the volume of the cylinder than the volume of the cone?

A. $\dfrac{1}{3}$

B. $\dfrac{1}{2}$

C. 2

D. 3

72.   A figure is shown on the grid below.

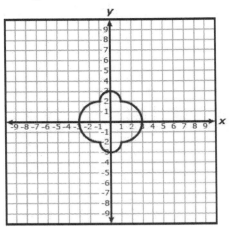

Which graph best represents this figure after it has been translated 5 units up and 3 units to the right?

F
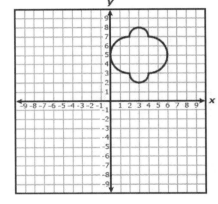

H
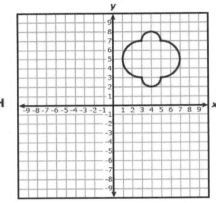

G
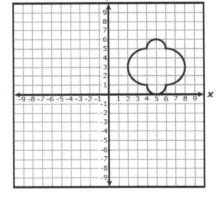

J
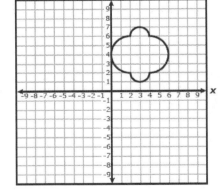

73.   Quadrilateral *ABCD* is a dilation of quadrilateral EFGH, with the origin as the center of dilation.

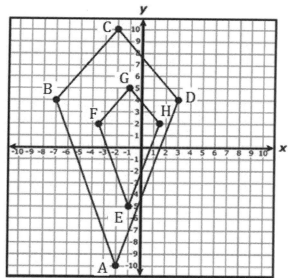

What appears to be the scale factor used to create this dilation?

A. 4

B. 0.5

C. 2

D. 0.25

74.   The graph of a figure is shown below.

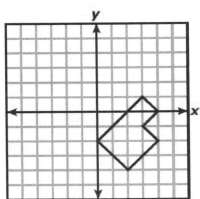

Which graph represents the reflection of this figure across the *x*-axis?

A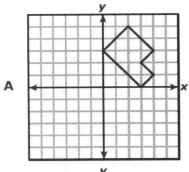

C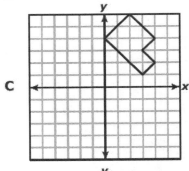

B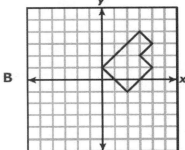

D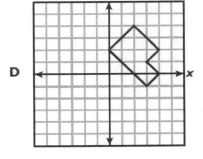

75. A figure is graphed on a coordinate grid as shown.

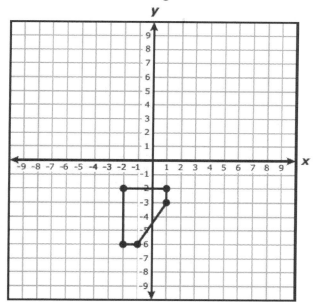

The figure is rotated 270° clockwise with the origin as the center of rotation to create a new figure. Which rule describes this transformation?

A. $(x, y) \rightarrow (-x, -y)$

B. $(x, y) \rightarrow (x, -y)$

C. $(x, y) \rightarrow (-y, x)$

D. $(x, y) \rightarrow (-x, y)$

76. Triangle *ABC* is a dilation of triangle *XYZ*.

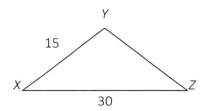 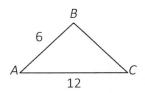

What scale factor was used to reduce *XYZ* to *ABC*?

A. 2.5

B. 0.8

C. 0.4

D. 0.2

77. Figure S, the small arrow, was dilated with the origin as the center of dilation to create Figure T, the large arrow.

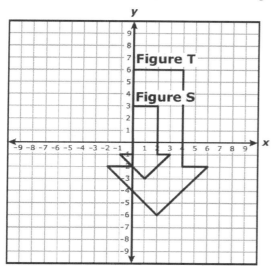

Which rule best represents the dilation that was applied to Figure S to create Figure T?

A. $(x, y) \rightarrow (2x, 2y)$

B. $(x, y) \rightarrow (4x, 4y)$

C. $(x, y) \rightarrow \left(\frac{1}{2}x, \frac{1}{2}y\right)$

D. $(x, y) \rightarrow \left(\frac{1}{4}x, \frac{1}{4}y\right)$

78.   Point *M* is located at (4, 6) on a coordinate grid. Point M is translated 8 units to the left and 9 units down to create point *M'*.

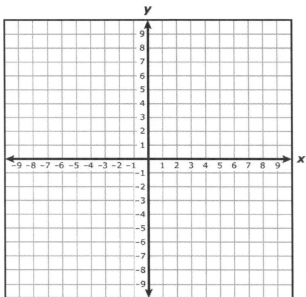

Which measurement is closest to the distance between point M and point M' in units?

A. 4 units

B. 17 units

C. 9 units

D. 12 units

79.   The coordinate grid shows parallelogram PQRS.

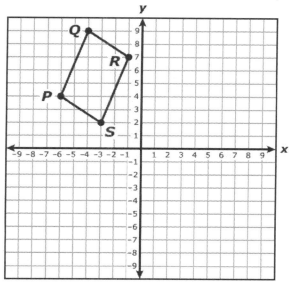

Parallelogram PQRS is rotated 90° clockwise about the origin to create parallelogram P'Q'R'S'. Which rule describes this transformation?

A. $(x, y) \rightarrow (x, -y)$

B. $(x, y) \rightarrow (-x, y)$

C. $(x, y) \rightarrow (y, x)$

D. $(x, y) \rightarrow (y, -x)$

80.   Triangles PQR and RST are similar right triangles.

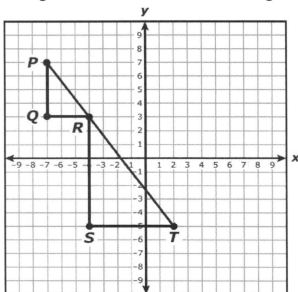

Which proportion can be used to show that the slope of $\overline{PR}$ is equal to the slope of $\overline{RT}$?

A. $\dfrac{3-7}{-4-(-7)} = \dfrac{-5-3}{2-(-4)}$

B. $\dfrac{3-(-4)}{7-(-7)} = \dfrac{-5-2}{3-(-4)}$

C. $\dfrac{-4-(-7)}{3-7} = \dfrac{2-(-4)}{-5-3}$

D. $\dfrac{-4-(-3)}{-7-7} = \dfrac{2-(-5)}{-4-3}$

81.   Circle I was dilated with the origin as the center of dilation to create Circle II.

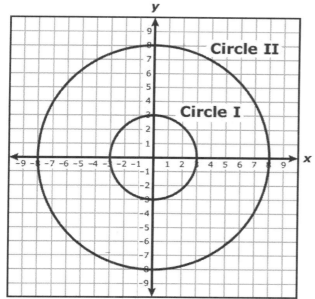

Which rule best represents the dilation applied to Circle I to create Circle II?

A. $(x, y) \rightarrow \left(\frac{3}{8}x, \frac{3}{8}y\right)$

B. $(x, y) \rightarrow \left(\frac{8}{3}x, \frac{8}{3}y\right)$

C. $(x, y) \rightarrow (x + 5, y + 5)$

D. $(x, y) \rightarrow (x - 5, y - 5)$

82.   Which representation of a transformation on a coordinate grid does not preserve congruence?

A. $(x, y) \rightarrow \left(\frac{1}{7}x, \frac{1}{7}y\right)$

B. $(x, y) \rightarrow (x + 7, y + 7)$

C. $(x, y) \rightarrow (x, y)$

D. $(x, y) \rightarrow (y, -x)$

83. Triangle *ABC* was translated 2 units to the right and 3 units down. Which rule describes the translation that was applied to triangle *ABC* to create triangle A'B'C'?

A. $(x, y) \rightarrow (x - 3, y + 2)$
B. $(x, y) \rightarrow (x + 2, y - 3)$
C. $(x, y) \rightarrow (2x, -3y)$
D. $(x, y) \rightarrow (-3x, 2y)$

84. Triangle *MNP* is graphed on a coordinate grid with vertices at *M*(−3, −6), *N*(0, 3) and *P*(6, −3). Triangle *MNP* is dilated by a scale factor of *u* with the origin as the center of dilation to create triangle *M'N'P'*; *u* >1

Which ordered pair represents the coordinates of the vertex *P'*?

A. $(6 + u, -3 + u)$
B. $\left(\dfrac{6}{u}, -\dfrac{3}{u}\right)$
C. $\left(6 + \dfrac{1}{u}, -3 + \dfrac{1}{u}\right)$
D. $(6u, -3u)$

85. Figure ABCDE is similar to figure VWXYZ.

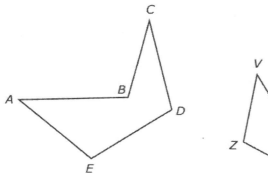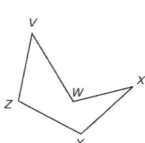

Which proportion must be true?

A. $\dfrac{AE}{XY} = \dfrac{CD}{VZ}$

B. $\dfrac{AB}{VW} = \dfrac{YZ}{DE}$

C. $\dfrac{BC}{XY} = \dfrac{DE}{YZ}$

D. $\dfrac{AB}{VW} = \dfrac{CD}{XY}$

86. Pentagon MNPQR is shown on the coordinate gird. Pentagon MNPQR is dilated with the origin as the center of dilation using the rule $(x, y) \rightarrow \left(\frac{1}{4}x, \frac{1}{4}y\right)$ to create pentagon $M'N'P'Q'R'$.

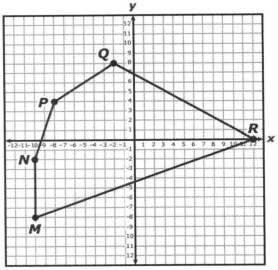

Which statement is true?

A. Pentagon $M'N'P'Q'R'$ is larger than pentagon MNPQR, because the scale factor is greater than 1.

B. Pentagon $M'N'P'Q'R'$ is smaller than pentagon MNPQR, because the scale factor is less than 1.

C. Pentagon $M'N'P'Q'R'$ is smaller than pentagon MNPQR, because the scale factor is greater than 1.

D. Pentagon $M'N'P'Q'R'$ is larger than pentagon MNPQR, because the scale factor is less than 1.

87.   A cone and its dimensions are shown in the diagram.

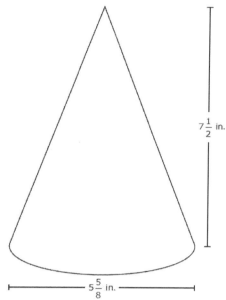

$7\frac{1}{2}$ in.

$5\frac{5}{8}$ in.

Which measurement is closest to the volume of the cone in cubic inches?

A. 186.38 in³

B. 248.50 in³

C. 745.51 in³

D. 62.13 in³

88.   A triangular prism and its dimensions are shown in the diagram.

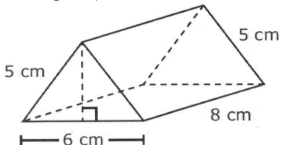

What is the lateral surface area of this triangular prism in square centimeters?

A. 192 cm²

B. 128 cm²

C. 152 cm²

D. 144 cm²

89.   A ball shaped like a sphere has a radius of 2.7 centimeters. Which measurement is closest to the volume of the ball in cubic centimeters?

A. 46.38 cm³

B. 33.93 cm³

C. 122.15 cm³

D. 82.45 cm³

90.   Four triangles are shown.

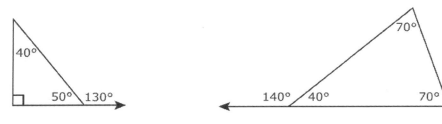

Based on these triangles, which statement is true?

A. $w = 75°$, because 45 + 60 = 105 and 180 − 105 = 75

B. $w = 105°$, because 180 − (45 + 60) = 75 and 180 − 75 = 105

C. $w = 285°$, because 45 + 60 = 105 and 105 + 180 = 285

D. $w = 165°$, because 180 − 60 = 120 and 120 + 45 = 165

91.   The measures of two angles are $(5x + 24)°$ and $(9x − 17)°$. What is the value of x if these angles are congruent?

A. 1.75

B. 13.2

C. 0.5

D. 10.25

92.   Triangle JKL is shown below

Note: picture not drawn to scale

If the measure of angle KLJ is five times the measure of angle JKL, which equation can be used to find the measure of angle JKL, *x*?

A. $5x + 90° = 360°$

B. $6x + 90° = 360°$

C. $5x + 90° = 180°$

D. $6x + 90° = 180°$

93.   In the figure below, AB is parallel to DC and BC is parallel to ED.

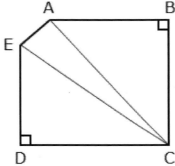

Note: picture not drawn to scale

If m∠DCB = 90°, m∠DCE = 37° and m∠BAC = 48°, what is m∠ECA?

A. 5°

B. 101°

C. 11°

D. 85°

94. In the figure below, m∠PDE = 38°, m∠APB = 73°, and m∠AED = 104° assuming it is regular pentagon.

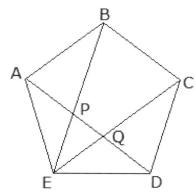

Note: picture not drawn to scale

What is m∠AEB?
A. 215°
B. 35°
C. 69°
D. 125°

95. If $m\angle 1 = (2x + 45)°$ and $m\angle 7 = (3x - 20)°$, what is $m\angle 2$?

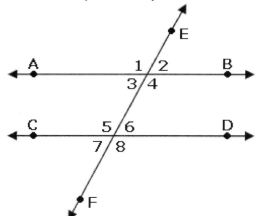

96.　In the figure below of a parallel lines cut by a transversal, which angle is supplementary to ∡8?

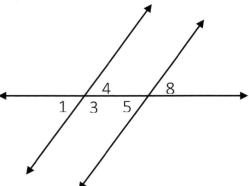

A.　∡1

B.　∡3

C.　∡4

D.　∡5

97. Glenda bought a holiday ornament in the shape of a rectangular pyramid, as shown below.

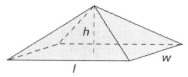

If l = 36 mm, h = 27 mm, and the ornament has a volume of 8,748 cu mm, what is the width of the ornament?
A. 9 mm
B. 3 mm
C. 8,748 mm
D. 27 m

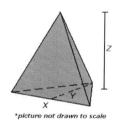

*picture not drawn to scale

98.

If X= 7 units, Y = 5 units, and Z = 12 units, what is the volume of the triangular pyramid shown above; assuming Y is height of triangular base?
A. 58.33 cubic units
B. 70 cubic units
C. 140 cubic units
D. 52.5 cubic units

99. A cylinder has height of 15 cm and a volume of 500 cm³. Calculate the radius of the cylinder. Round your answer to the nearest hundredth.

100.   Christina folds the net below into a cube.

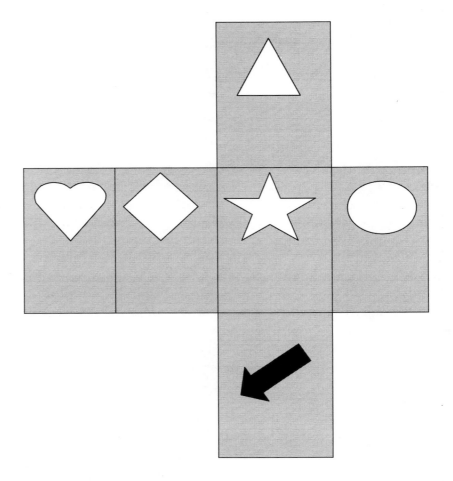

Which figure shows the cube?

A.   C.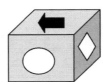

B.   D.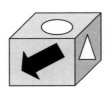

Answer Key

		Marks (C/W)			Marks (C/W)			Marks (C/W)
1	B		35	B		69	B	
2	24		36	C		70	A	
3	B		37	C		71	D	
4	C		38	A		72	F	
5	12.96		39	D		73	C	
6	22.26		40	D		74	D	
7	C		41	C		75	C	
8	B		42	B		76	C	
9	20		43	C		77	A	
10	B		44	A		78	D	
11	D		45	B		79	D	
12	D		46	C		80	A	
13	D		47	A		81	B	
14	B		48	C		82	A	
15	C		49	H		83	B	
16	C		50	D		84	D	
17	B		51	B		85	D	
18	D		52	C		86	B	
19	B		53	B		87	D	
20	C		54	D		88	B	
21	D		55	D		89	D	
22	C		56	A		90	B	
23	A		57	C		91	D	
24	B		58	A		92	D	
25	C		59	D		93	C	
26	C		60	D		94	B	
27	B		61	B		95	73	
28	B		62	D		96	B	
29	D		63	D		97	D	
30	B		64	A		98	B	
31	D		65	A		99	3.26	
32	D		66	B		100	B	
33	C		67	A		101		
34	D		68	C		102		
	Total			Total			Total	

SECTION 4

DATA ANALYSIS, PROBABILITY AND FINANCIAL LITERACY

1. The number of students in each of the 2 exercise classes are same. The box and whisker plots below represent the average amount of time spent exercising on daily in the outdoor class.

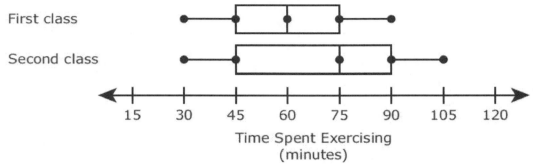

Based on the information in the box and whisker plots, which statement relating to the time spent exercising in the outdoor class appears to be true?

A. The median amount of time the first class spent exercising was greater than the median amount of time the second class spent exercising.

B. The range for the second class was less than the range for the first class.

C. The interquartile range for the first class was less than the interquartile range for the second class.

D. The minimum amount of time the second class spent exercising was greater than the minimum amount of time the first class spent exercising.

2. The director of a middle school play wants to find out how many students at the school plan to watch the play on the opening night. Which sampling method is most likely to provide valid results?

A. Surveying 2 randomly chosen students from each of the 25 homeroom classes in the school

B. Surveying 50 randomly chosen students from eighth grade

C. Surveying 5 randomly chosen students from each of the 10 art classes in the school

D. Surveying 10 randomly chosen students reading in the library during 5 different lunch periods

3. The scatter plot below shows movie theaters with different numbers of screens and their average weekly attendance.

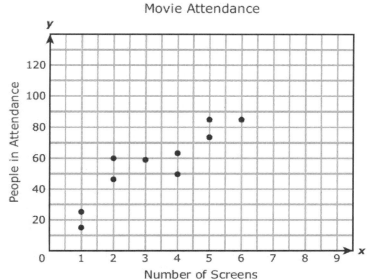

Movie Attendance

Based on the trend in the scatter plot, approximately how many people will be in attendance at a movie theater with 8 screens?

A. 90

B. 105

C. 85

D. 140

4. A store manager discounted the pricing of several items during a sale. The original price and the sale price of each item are shown in the table below.

Store Sale

Original Price	Sale Price
$30	$24
$40	$32
$50	$40
$60	$48
$70	$56

Based on the data in the table, what would be the sale price of an item that had an original price of $85?

A. $79
B. $64
C. $68
D. $71

5. Samina's science test score for the first quarter is 50, 50, 79, 82, 83, and 84. Which measure would show the highest result?

A. Mean
B. Median
C. Mode
D. Range

6. The table shows the lunch choices of students for one day.

Lunch	Number of Students
Garlic Sandwich	35
Chicken Sandwich	49
Pasta	55
Soup	32
Veggie Burger	23

Which of the following conclusion is supported by the data?
A. Garlic sandwich was the favorite lunch that day.

B. More students ate pasta than soup or veggie burger.

C. Students will eat more veggie burgers than soup the next day.

D. Twice as many students ate chicken sandwiches than pasta.

7. Ricky read an article in the local newspaper which stated that the city park levy was expected to pass in the next election. Ricky surveyed the people in his neighborhood and gathered the following data.

Survey Results for Ricky' Neighborhood	
Vote	Number
For the Park Levy	28
Against the Park Levy	71

From these results, Ricky concluded that the newspaper article was incorrect. Which one is the best explanation for why this conclusion might not be reasonable?
A. The sample does not represent all of the voters in the city.

B. The sample size is too large.

C. The newspaper surveys are always reliable.

D. The data collector is biased.

8. Greenhouse gas emissions are blamed for excess pollution and potential long-term global warming. Greenhouse gases come from four main sources. The table shows the breakdown.

Source	Greenhouse Emissions (in%)
Nitrous Oxide	7.0%
Methane	8.6%
Carbon Dioxide	83.4%
HFC's, PFC's, Sulfur	3.0%

Which circle graph best represents the same information?

A.

Nitrous Oxide | Methane

HFC's PFC's Sulfur | Carbon Dioxide

C.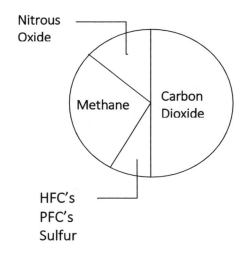

B.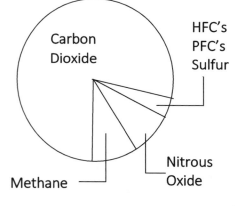

D.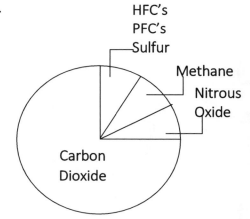

9.   The science test score for 20 students is listed below.

48, 49, 50, 46, 47, 47, 35, 38, 40, 42, 45, 47, 48, 44, 43, 46, 45, 42, 43, 47

Which of the display matches this data?

A.

B.

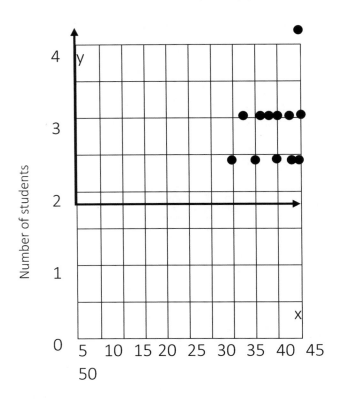

Test Score

C.

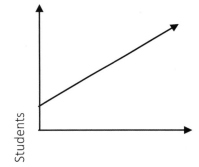

Test Score

D.

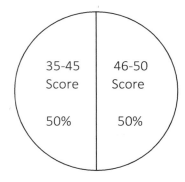

10. The students in Mr. Henry's mathematics class wanted to find out which restaurant in the town is liked most by the City's residents. Students took turns, standing outside the Mexican Restaurant to survey customers as they left the restaurant. Out of the 300 people surveyed, 223 said that Mexican restaurant was their most favorite place to eat. From the survey results, the class concluded that the Mexican restaurant was the most favorite place of all city's residents. Which one is the best explanation for why this conclusion might NOT be valid?

A. The sample was biased.

B. The sample was not random.

C. The sample size was too small.

D. The sample size was too large.

11. A local newspaper wants to find out the opinions of city residents regarding a new senior center. In order to do this, the newspaper's editor plans to survey a random sample of adult residents. From which of these listings should the editor draw the names of people to survey?

A. City and county workers

B. Small business association

C. Members of the senior health clinic

D. The local telephone directory

12. Jenifer surveyed people leaving a recycling center to determine the attitudes of Americans toward ground and water pollution. Which one is the best explanation of why the results of this survey might NOT be valid?

A. The survey did not consider attitudes of people in other countries.

B. Participants were not surveyed by mail or on the phone.

C. The sample was not representative of the population to which he generalized.

D. The survey was carried out by a student.

13. The members of the Patts Middle School Student Council passed out a questionnaire to all 900 students, asking about the students' lunch preferences. Out of the 28 students who returned the survey, 18 said that they would like to have outside restaurants sell food in the cafeteria. Based on the results, the student council concluded that most of the students want restaurant food available in the cafeteria. Why might the conclusion NOT be valid?
   A. The sample was not random.
   B. The sample group did not represent the whole population.
   C. The sample size was too small.
   D. The sample size was too large.

14. The bar graph shows the average number of hours that people in different age groups spend watching television each week.

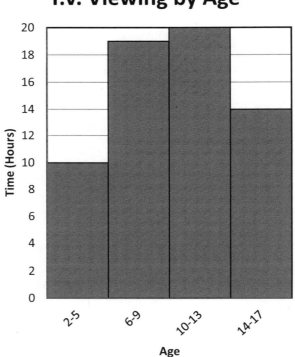

T.V. Viewing by Age

Which statement best explains why the graph could be misleading?
   A. The age intervals are too wide spread.
   B. The title of the graph is misleading.
   C. The intervals on the vertical scale are not uniform.
   D. The bar length do not correctly reflect the data.

15. John's father is a manager. He is comparing the salaries of the workers in his department to the industry's average salary of $30,000. The table shows the information he collected.

Employee	Salary
John's father (boss)	$109,000
Christine	$24,000
Sam	$23,000
Mike	$26,000
Lynn	$28,000

John's father determines that the average salary in the department is $42,000, well above the industry average. Why is the conclusion made by John's father is misleading?

A. $42,000 is the mean, which is misleading since John's father's salary is so much higher than the other employees.

B. $42,000 is the range of the salaries rather than an average salary. He calculated incorrectly.

C. $42,000 is the median salary rather than the mean salary. He calculated incorrectly.

D. He did not verify the industry average, and so cannot claim that the salaries of his employees are well above the industry average.

16. The table displays the number of contacts six people have stored in their cell phone.

Cell Phone Contacts

Person	Number of Contacts
Mary	68
Wes	72
Keith	77
Julie	64
Anthony	69
Lan	76

What is the mean absolute deviation for this set of data?

A. 71

B. 24

C. 4

D. 13

17. A survey is conducted to find the favorite food among eighth-grade students at Franklin Middle School. Which of the following sampling methods would give the most accurate result?

A. Survey every eight-grade student whose name begins with a vowel.

B. Survey every eighth-grade student and his or her parents.

C. Survey every other eighth-grade girl as she comes into the cafeteria.

D. Survey every eighth-grade student who participates in sports.

18. Sam separated his restaurant coupons into different categories. The table at the right shows the number of coupons he has for each type of restaurant.

Type of Restaurant	Coupons
Mexican	15
Chinese	12
Indian	4
Italian	16
German	3

If Diego selects a coupon at random, what is the probability that he will select a Mexican restaurant coupon?

A. 0.15
B. 0.35
C. 0.30
D. 0.75

19. A dude ranch in Odessa records the number of visitors at the ranch each month. The graph below shows the number of visitors over the last 6 months.

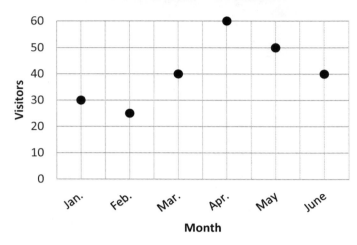

Dude Ranch Visitors

Which measure of central tendency would make the number of visitors appear to be the highest?

A. Mean

B. Median

C. Mode

D. Range

20. The table below states the average cost per semester paid by a student of University of Texas. Which of the following conclusion is correct based on the data in the table?

University of Texas Per Semester Cost	
Tuition	$3,512
Books	$400
Room/board	$3,819
Transportation	$425
Miscellaneous	$1,075
Total	$9,231

A. Tuition is more than half of the cost per semester.

B. Miscellaneous expenses are less than 10% of the cost per semester.

C. Tuition and room and board are more than 75% of the cost per semester.

D. The cost of books is included with tuition.

21. Lehman surveyed all the members of her horse-riding club regarding their favorite after-school activity. The results are shown in the table.

Favorite After-School Activity	
Activity	Number of Students
Watching T.V.	2
Eating	3
Playing Video Games	1
Doing Homework	2
Playing Outside	5
Sports	15

Out of these results, Lehman concluded that sports were the most favorite after-school activity of students in her town. Which is the best explanation for why her conclusion might not be valid?

A. The survey was not conducted by an adult.

B. The sample was not representative of all of the students in her town.

C. The survey was not done by telephone.

D. The survey did not involve parents.

22. The population density in Texas is 84.5, which means that an average of 84.5 people lives in each square mile. According to the average, how many people live in 750 square miles?

   A. 634

   B. 8,432

   C. 63,375

   D. 640,000

23. The spinner at the bottom is divided into six equal sections. The spinner was spun 84 times. The total number of times the spinner landed on each number is shown in the table below.

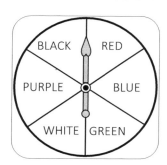

Color	Frequency
Red	15
Blue	20
Green	7
White	8
Purple	15
Black	19

Based on the theoretical probability, how many times should the spinner land on WHITE in 84 spins?

   A. 4

   B. 6

   C. 8

   D. 14

24. The table displays the ages of two groups of senior citizens who reside at a nursing care center.

Group 1	65	70	70	71	75	85	88	89	90
Group 2	62	70	70	76	81	84	85	86	87

Which measure of central tendency has a greater value of Group 1 than Group 2?

A. Mean

B. Median

C. Mode

D. Range

25. Madonna analyzed the graph below and determined that the mode of the number of lunches sold during the week was 400. Which statement is true?

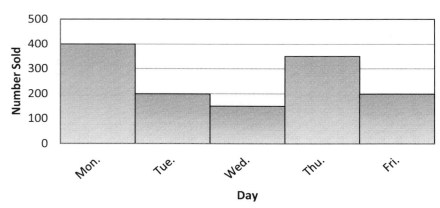

Cafeteria Lunch Sales

A. Madonna's conclusion is correct.

B. The actual mode is 200.

C. The mean is 300.

D. The collection of data is biased.

26. The scatterplot shows the number of digital cameras sold each year at a photography store.

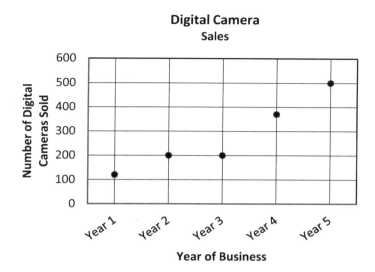

Digital Camera Sales

Which description best represents the relationship in the data?

A. No trend

B. Positive trend

C. Negative tend

D. Both positive and negative trend

27. Simpson used a local telephone directory to randomly choose 8 people to survey about a new park. All 8 people said that they were in favor of the new park. Which is the best explanation for why her conclusion might not be valid?

A. The sample was not representative of all of the people in her town.

B. The sample size was too small.

C. The survey population was too large.

D. The survey was conducted by telephone.

28. There are 40 newborn babies in the hospital nursery. For every 3 girls, there are 2 boys. How many newborn boys are in the nursery?

    A. 7

    B. 12

    C. 16

    D. 18

29. Scientists are studying a problem regarding enormous number of fruit flies in an orchard. The following results were generated.

Day	1	2	3	4	5
Number of Fruit Flies	256	1,024	4,096	16,384	65,536

    How can the data best be described?

    A. The number of fruit flies doubles daily.

    B. The number of fruit flies quadruples daily.

    C. The number of fruit flies increases by a power of 2 daily.

    D. The number of fruit flies increases by 4 daily.

30.   Krista set up a monthly budget, as represented by the circle graph below.

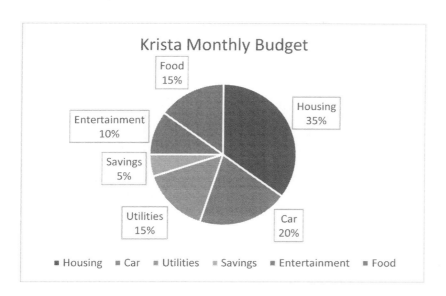

Which conclusion is NOT supported by the circle graph?

A. Krista spends 50% of her income on housing and food.

B. Krista spends 25% of her income on her car and utilities.

C. Krista spends 50% of her income on housing and utilities.

D. Krista spends 25% of her income on food and entertainment.

31. Bianca purchased some art supplies and cardstock to make greeting cards. The graph below displays the relationship between the number of greeting cards Bianca made and the total cost accrued of the materials used to design the cards.

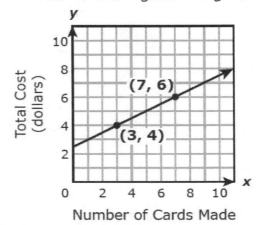

Cost of Making Greeting Cards

Based on the graph, what will be the total cost of making 25 greeting cards?

A. $12.50

B. $50.00

C. $52.50

D. $15.00

32. The scatterplot below shows the relationship between the daily high temperature and the number of snow cones sold at a concession stand on a given day.

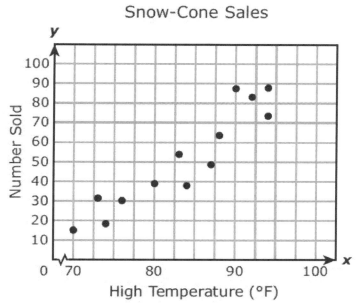

Snow-Cone Sales

Based on the scatterplot, approximately how many snow cones will be sold on a day when the high temperature is 82°F?

A. 63

B. 46

C. 29

D. 33

33. The ages of the members of a volunteer group are shown below.

13, 14, 14, 14, 15, 15, 15, 16, 16, 21, 23

Which box and whisker plot best represents this data?

A.

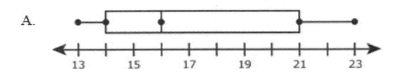

B.

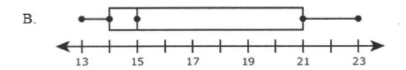

C.

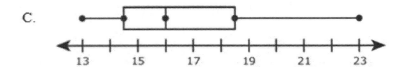

D.

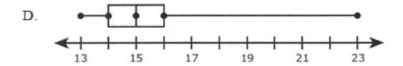

34. Ted created a graph to exhibit the percentage of time he spends on different activities during a school week day.

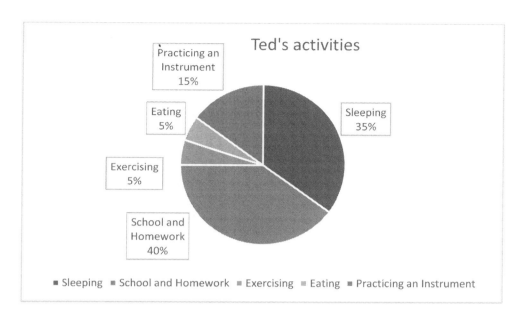

Ted concluded from the graph that he spends about 48 hours at school and completing homework during a five-day school week. Which statement about Ted's conclusion is true?

A. Ted's conclusion is invalid because $\frac{1}{4}$ of 120 is 30.

B. Ted's conclusion is invalid because 40% of 24 are 9.6.

C. Ted's conclusion is valid because 40% of 120 are 48.

D. Ted's conclusion is valid because $\frac{1}{4}$ of 192 is 48.

35. The graph below displays the number of books sold at a book fair in 5 days.

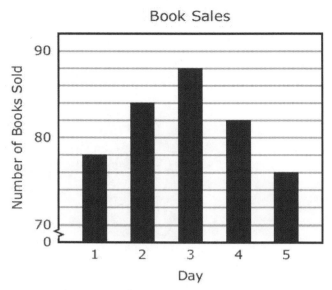

Based on the graph, which statement is true?

A. The number of books sold on Day 3 was twice the number of books sold on Day1.

B. The number of books sold on Day 5 was half the number of books sold on Day 2.

C. The number of books sold on Day 5 was about 93% of the number of books sold on Day 4.

D. The number of books sold on Day 1 was about 12% of the number of books sold on Day 3.

36. Tickets were sold at four different gates of a high school football stadium. The graph below shows the percentage of the total tickets sold at each gate during a recent game.

Ticket Sales

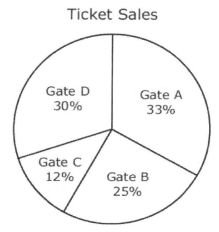

If 90 tickets were sold at Gate C, what was the total number of tickets sold?

A. 750

B. 1,080

C. 360

D. 1,168

37. Lily conducted a survey of her classmates in which she asked each student to choose his or her favorite cafeteria lunch. She listed her results in the table below.

Favorite Lunch Item	Number of Students
Hamburger	5
Noodles	9
Turkey sandwich	4
Pasta	4
Salad	3
Other	5

If she wants to create a circle graph, highlighting the percentage of students who chose each type of lunch, what will be the degree measure of the sector labeled "Noodles"?

A. 154°

B. 108°

C. 30°

D. 9°

38.   The graph below exhibits the annual sales for Ricks's Savory Snacks since 1985. Based on the data shown in the graph, which is the best prediction for sales in the year 2015?

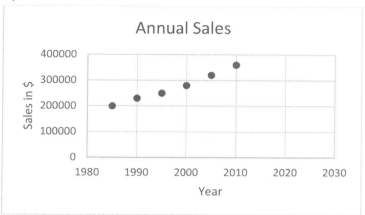

A. $500, 000

B. $450, 000

C. $400, 000

D. $350, 000

39. Which scatters plot displays the relationship between the number of gallons of gasoline remaining in a motorcycle's tank and the number of miles driven since the tank was filled?

A.

B.

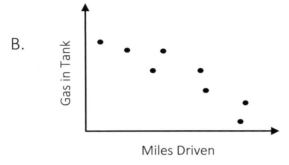

C.

D.

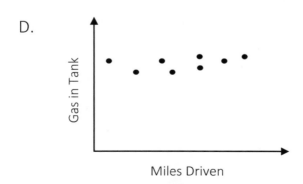

40. A shoe store recorded the number of each type of shoe sold during the past month. The data is presented in the table shown. What type of graph would best represent the number of shoes sold by type?

Type of Shoe	Pairs Sold
Loafers	39
Tennis shoes	41
Sandals	59
High heels	15
Work boots	8
Winter boots	5
Walking shoes	28

A. Histogram
B. Bar graph
C. Circle graph
D. Scatterplot

41.   Jonas's older sister works at a computer store. She wants to ask her boss for a raise, so she creates a graph to emphasize how her computer sales have increased over the past six months.

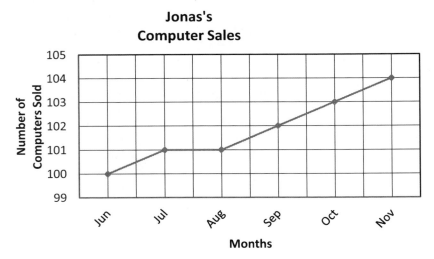

The boss thinks that Jonas's graph is misleading. Which of the following best explains why the graph is misleading?

A. The intervals are not uniform on the y-axis.

B. The data set is too small.

C. The intervals on the y-axis make the increase in sales appear significant.

D. The data should be displayed as a circle graph rather than a line graph.

42.   Pondrick plotted a part of downtown Dallas on a coordinate grid displaying each intersection as an ordered pair. Pondrick started at the center of the town, which she plotted at the origin. Then she moved two blocks north, two blocks east, and two blocks south. Which ordered pair shows her location on the grid?

A. (2, -2)

B. (0, 2)

C. (2, 0)

D. (2, 4)

43. Ruby can decorate 3 cakes in 5 hours. Which graph has a slope that best represents the number of cakes per hour Ruby can decorate?

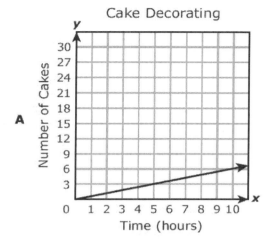

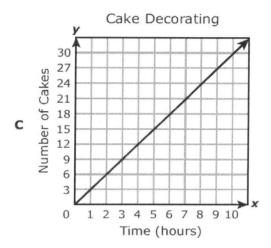

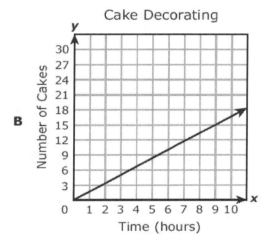

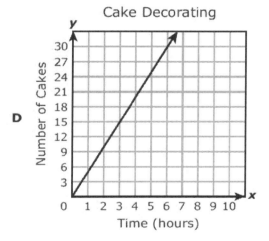

44. Mrs. Phillips created a scatterplot to display the relationship between the number of absences a student in her class has and the student's final exam score.

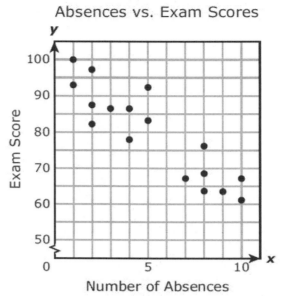

Based on this scatterplot, approximately what score should a student with 6 absences expect to receive on the final exam?

A. 65

B. 92

C. 67

D. 76

45. The list below shows the high temperatures for 8 days in April in Fort Worth, Texas.

70°F 80°F 62°F 93°F

68°F 87°F 73°F 87°F

Which histogram correctly displays the information?

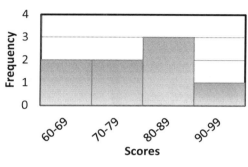

A.

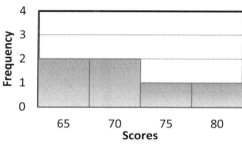

B.

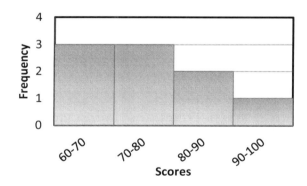

C.

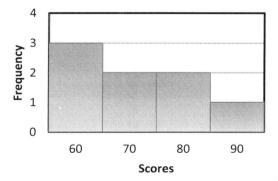

D.

46. Mrs. Kennedy conducted a survey to determine the number of pets that each of her students has. The data appear in the table below.

Number of Pets	Number of Students with This Many Pets
0	12
1	6
2	3
3	3

Which of the following circle graphs best represents the data in the table?

A. Comparison of Students by Number of Pets

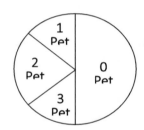

B. Comparison of Students by Number of Pets

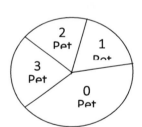

C. Comparison of Students by Number of Pets

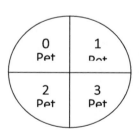

D. Comparison of Students by Number of Pets

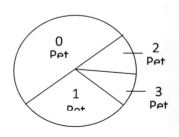

47. The table below highlights a company's charitable donations for the years 2002 to 2006.

Year	Annual Donation
2002	$50,000
2003	$55,000
2004	$61,000
2005	$65,000
2006	$70,000

Which bar graph matches the data in the table?

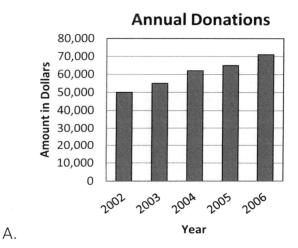

A.

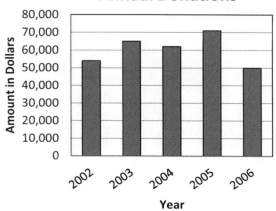

B.

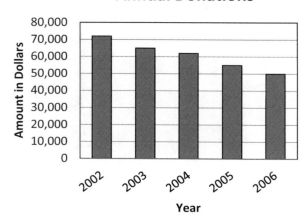

C.

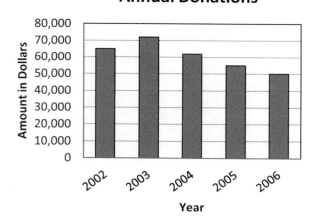

D.

48. Which statement best explains why a person reading the circle graph would get an incorrect idea about the number of students who prefer certain fruits?

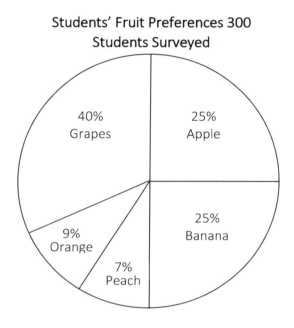

Students' Fruit Preferences 300
Students Surveyed

40%
Grapes

25%
Apple

9%
Orange

7%
Peach

25%
Banana

A. The title is misleading.

B. The section labeling is unclear.

C. The circle graph is missing a scale.

D. The sum of percentages for all sections is greater than 100.

49.   An eighth-grade student estimated that she needs $11000 for tuition and fees for each year of college. She already has $6,000 in her savings account. The table shows the projected future value of the account in five years based on different monthly deposits.

Future Value of a Savings Account

Initial Balance (dollars)	6,000	6,000	6,000	6,000
Monthly Deposit (dollars)	100	200	300	400
Account Value in Five Years (dollars)	12,000	18,000	24,000	30,000

The student wants to have enough money saved in five years to pay the tuition and fees for her first three years of college. Based on the table, what is the minimum amount she should deposit in the savings account every month?

A. 325
B. 300
C. 350
D. 400

50.   Mr. Davis opened an account with a deposit of $50,000.
   • The account earned annual simple interest.
   • He did not make any additional deposits or withdrawals.
   At the end of 4 years, the balance of the account was $65,000. Calculate the annual interest rate on this account?

51. Mr. Tiago asked his students to name their favorite math tool or object. The table below shows the results.

Favorite Math Tool or Object	
Tool or Object	Number of Students
Ruler	13
Compass	50
Protractor	25
Tangram	12

Which graph best represents the data?

A.

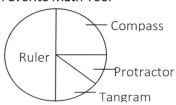

B.

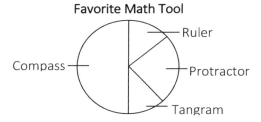

C.

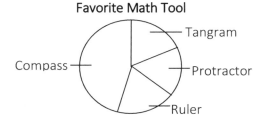

D.

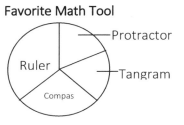

52. The chart below shows basketball shots attempted and made by four players on the team.

Name	Shots Attempted	Shots Made
Alan	16	5
Ben	12	7
Carter	10	4
Davin	9	4

Which of the following lists the players in order from highest to lowest percentage of shots made out of the shots attempted?

A. Ben, Davin, Carter, Alan

B. Alan, Carter, Davin, Ben

C. Davin, Carter, Ben Alan

D. Ben, Carter Alan, Davin

53. An investor deposits $5,500 into a life insurance policy that pays 2.5% simple annual interest. If no additional investment is made into the policy, how much accumulated interest should the investor expect at the end of 10 years?

   A. 6,775

   B. 6,875

   C. 1,375

   D. None of the above

54. Adam invests $5,000.00 in a retirement account that offers 3% interest compounded annually. He makes no additional deposits or withdrawals. Which amount is closest to the interest he will have earned at the end of 5 years?

   A. 700

   B. 750

   C. 800

   D. 850

55. Mr. Martin deposited $25,000 in a new account at his bank.
    • The bank pays 5.5% interest compounded annually on this account.
    • Mr. Martin makes no additional deposits or withdrawals.
    Which amount is closest to the balance of the account at the end of 3 years?
    A. 29,000
    B. 29,350
    C. 30,000
    D. 4,300

56. The total cost of attending a state university is $21,000 for the first year. A student's parents will pay half of this cost. A merit scholarship will pay another $5,000. Which amount is closest to the minimum that the student will need to save every month to pay off the remaining cost at the end of 12 months?
    A. 400
    B. 450
    C. 460
    D. 500

57. Melisa requires a $25,000 loan to purchase home improvement articles. Which loan option would allow her to pay the least amount of interest?
    A An 18-month loan with a 4.75% annual simple interest rate.
    B A 30-month loan with a 3.00% annual simple interest rate.
    C A 24-month loan with a 4.00% annual simple interest rate.
    D A 36-month loan with a 2.00% annual simple interest rate.

58. The list represents the heights of 6 students in inches.
    63, 70, 68, 73, 58, 67
    What is the mean absolute deviation for these numbers?
    A. 3
    B. 3.5
    C. 4
    D. 4.5

59. The list below exhibits the number of songs that five students each downloaded last week.

32, 43, 38, 28, 51

What is the mean absolute deviation of the numbers in the list?

    A. 6.88

    B. 5.98

    C. 7.08

    D. 6.68

60. Teena has $850 to deposit into two different savings accounts.

  • She deposited $400 into a savings account, which earns 3.5% annual simple interest.

  • She also deposited $450 into another savings account, which earns 3.0% interest compounded annually.

Teena will not make any additional deposits or withdrawals. Which amount is closest to the total balance of these two accounts at the end of 3 years?

    A. 932.5

    B. 933.73

    C. 935.2

    D. None of above

61. Alexandra and her family are discussing how to pay for her college education. The cost of tuition at the college that Alexandra wants to attend is $19,000 per year. Alexandra's parents will pay 80% of the tuition cost every year, and she will pay the rest. Alexandra has one year to save enough money to attend her first year of college. What is the minimum amount of money she should save every month to reach her goal?

62. Ben has a coin and a number cube. The number cube is labeled 1 through 6. He flips the coin once and rolls the number cube once. What is the probability that the coin lands tails-up and the cube lands on an even number?

a. 2/3

b. ¼

c. 1/12

d. 1/6

63. Tony has 12 coins in his pocket. Out of these coins, 8 were made in the year 2000, and remaining 4 were made in the year 2005. Tony randomly selects one coin from his pocket, and without replacing it, he selects another coin from his pocket. What is the probability that both coins he selected were made in the year 2000?

a. 14/33

b. 4/9

c. 7/33

d. 2/9

64. Lisa has two cups containing different-colored paper clips. The first cup contains 7 pink and 3 green paper clips. The second cup contains 3 black, 1 red, and 6 white paper clips. What is the probability that Lisa will randomly select a green paper clip from the first cup and white paper clip from the second cup?

A. 7/8

B. 9/10

C. 9/14

D. 9/50

65.   For a school carnival, Mia creates a game involving the spinners below.

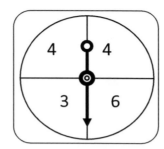 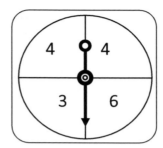

A contestant plays the game by first choosing one of the four rules listed below and then spinning the spinner. Which rule should a contestant choose to have the greatest chance of winning a prize?

A. Win a prize if the product is greater than 25.

B. Win a prize if the product is odd.

C. Win a prize if the sum is less than 3.

D. Win a prize if the sum or the product is 10.

66.   The spinner below is divided into 8 equal sections.

How many sections of the spinner should be colored red to make the probability of the arrow landing on red 0.375 in a single spin?

A. 1

B. 3

C. 5

D. 7

67.   The table shows the ages of two groups of citizens who reside at a nursing care center.

Group 1	60	68	70	71	75	85	88	88	65
Group 2	62	69	70	76	76	84	85	86	87

Which measure of central tendency has a greater value of Group 1 than Group 2?

   A. Mean
   B. Mode
   C. Median
   D. Range

68.   Disha is researching her family tree. She has made a temple for recording the names of her ancestors. How many people will be represented in the 5th generation before her?

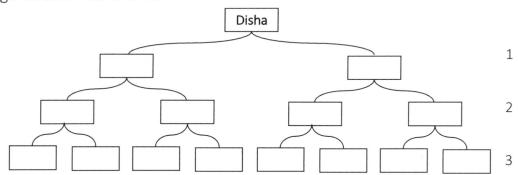

   A. 24
   B. 48
   C. 32
   D. 56

69. In a number cube game, the object is to roll three 6's. If a player rolls three number cubes, what is the probability of rolling three 6's?

F. $\dfrac{1}{2}$

G. $\dfrac{1}{6}$

H. $\dfrac{1}{36}$

J. $\dfrac{1}{216}$

70. A movie theater recorded the number of tickets sold daily for a popular movie during the month of June. The box-and-whisker plot shown below represents the data for the number of tickets sold, in hundreds.

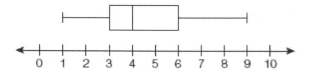

Which conclusion can be made using this plot?

A. The second quartile is 600.

B. The mean of the attendance is 400.

C. The range of the attendance is 300 to 600.

D. Twenty-five percent of the attendance is between 300 and 400.

71.　The data set 5, 6, 7, 8, 9, 9, 9, 10, 12, 14, 17, 17, 18, 19, 19 represents the number of hours spent on the Internet in a week by students in a mathematics class. Which box-and-whisker plot represents the data?

A.

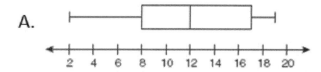

B.

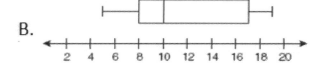

C.

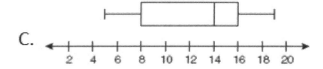

D.

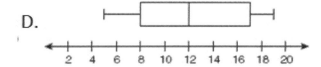

72. The accompanying box-and-whisker plots can be used to compare the annual incomes of three professions.

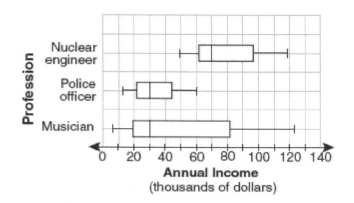

Based on the box-and-whisker plots, which statement is true?
   A. The median income for nuclear engineers is greater than the income of all musicians.
   B. The median income for police officers and musicians is the same.
   C. All nuclear engineers earn more than all police officers.
   D. A musician will eventually earn more than a police officer.

73. The accompanying stem-and-leaf plot represents Ben's test scores this year.

6	5	8				
7	2	3	3	3	3	9
8	1	3	3	6	7	
9	6	9	9			

Key: 7 | 2 = 72

What is the median score for this set of data?
   A. 73
   B. 80
   C. 79
   D. 81

74. George made the accompanying stem-and-leaf plot of the weights, in pounds, of each member of the wrestling team he was coaching.

Stem	Leaf
10	9
11	
12	3 8
13	2 4 4 6 8
14	1 3 5 5 9
15	2 3 7 7 9
16	1 3 7 8 8 8 9
17	3 8

Key: 16 | 1 = 161

What is the mode of the weights?

A. 145

B. 152

C. 150

D. 168

75. For their spring vacation, Leah's family has decided to go to one Texas beach, one Texas state park, and one professional sporting event in Houston. Their beach choices are South Padre Island, Crystal Beach, or Sunrise Beach. The state park choices are Copper Breaks State Park or Lake Rita Blanca State Park. The sports choices are a Houston Rockets basketball game or a Houston Astros baseball game. Which tree diagram shows all the possible combinations for the family vacation?

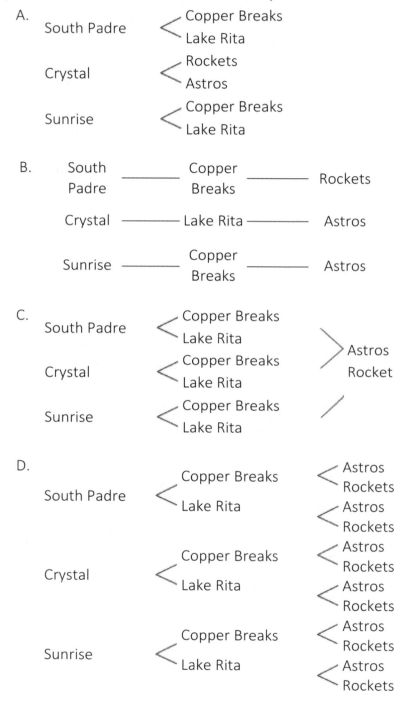

Answer Key

		Marks (C/W)
1	C	
2	A	
3	B	
4	C	
5	B	
6	B	
7	A	
8	B	
9	A	
10	A	
11	D	
12	C	
13	C	
14	B	
15	A	
16	C	
17	A	
18	C	
19	A	
20	C	
21	B	
22	C	
23	D	
24	A	
25	B	
26	B	
27	B	
28	C	
29	B	
30	B	
31	D	
32	B	
Total		

		Marks (C/W)
33	D	
34	C	
35	C	
36	A	
37	B	
38	C	
39	B	
40	B	
41	C	
42	B	
43	A	
44	D	
45	A	
46	D	
47	A	
48	D	
49	C	
50	7.50%	
51	B	
52	A	
53	C	
54	C	
55	B	
56	C	
57	D	
58	C	
59	A	
60	B	
61	317	
62	B	
63	A	
64	D	
Total		

		Marks (C/W)
65	D	
66	B	
67	B	
68	C	
69	J	
70	D	
71	B	
72	B	
73	B	
74	D	
75	D	
76		
77		
78		
79		
80		
81		
82		
83		
84		
85		
86		
87		
88		
89		
90		
91		
92		
93		
94		
95		
96		
	Total	

Made in the USA
Coppell, TX
12 April 2025

48191168R00125